ACES OF *JAGDSTAFFEL* 17

SERIES EDITOR: TONY HOLMES

OSPREY AIRCRAFT OF THE ACES 118

ACES OF *JAGDSTAFFEL* 17

Greg VanWyngarden

OSPREY
PUBLISHING

Front Cover
'I think a fighter pilot needs three things – guts, calmness and some luck. Guts to approach the enemy, calmness while firing and luck not to get shot down while doing so'. This was the simple yet effective philosophy of Julius Buckler, the most successful ace of the fighter squadron known as Royal Prussian *Jagdstaffel* 17.

On 12 May 1917, the 23-year-old Hessian NCO from Mainz would once again demonstrate those qualities. Buckler was already the leading scorer of his unit with six victories under his belt, all of them achieved while flying against the French. Three of those had been claimed in the preceding month of 'Bloody April' during the aerial action that accompanied French Gen Robert Nivelle's disastrous offensive known as the Second Battle of the Aisne. However, as the offensive lost its momentum in May the pace of aerial activity had also slackened. Buckler wrote that, 'Our sector of the front fell more and more quietly asleep. May of 1917 was the most calm and peaceful May of the war'.

Nevertheless, Buckler's luck once again proved itself as he stalked the skies over the Aisne on the evening of 12 May. Flying his trusted Albatros D III 2033/16 – prominently labelled *Mops* on the fuselage, as were all of his fighters – Buckler found the Nieuport 23 of Adjutant Albin Jaussaud of the *Escadrille* N75, flying over La Malmaison at about 1840 hrs. Buckler's attack forced the Frenchman lower and lower until he landed behind German lines. Jaussaud almost brought his Nieuport down successfully, but it overturned at the last moment with very minor damage. Buckler and his comrades would pose happily for photographs with the inverted trophy, together with a large number of curious onlookers. It was yet another memorable triumph for the aggressive pilots of *Jagdstaffel* 17 (*Cover artwork by Mark Postlethwaite*)

First published in Great Britain in 2013 by Osprey Publishing
Osprey Publishing, PO Box 883, Oxford, OX1 9PL, UK
Osprey Publishing, PO Box 3985, New York, NY 10185-3985, USA

E-mail: info@ospreypublishing.com

Osprey Publishing is part of the Osprey Group

A CIP catalogue record for this book is available from the British Library

ISBN: 978 1 78096 718 9
PDF e-book ISBN: 978 1 78096 720 2
ePub ISBN: 9781780967196

Edited by Tony Holmes
Cover Artwork by Mark Postlethwaite
Aircraft Profiles by Harry Dempsey
Index by Sandra Shotter
Originated by PDQ Digital Media Solutions, UK
Printed in China through Asia Pacific Offset Limited

13 14 15 16 17 10 9 8 7 6 5 4 3 2 1

Osprey Publishing is supporting the Woodland Trust, the UK's leading woodland conservation charity, by funding the dedication of trees.

www.ospreypublishing.com

CONTENTS

ORIGINS IN METZ

R oyal Prussian *Jagdstaffel* 17 was hardly the most famous or accomplished of the fighter units of the German Army Air Service in the Great War, but it did produce its share of successful aces in addition to some very distinctive characters. If one includes the men who flew in the ancestral 'core' or nuclear unit of the *Jasta* – the so-called *Kampfstaffel* Metz – then the ranks of this formation included three eventual knights of the *Orden Pour le Mérite*, or the 'Blue Max'. Foremost among these was Julius Buckler, the top-scoring pilot of *Jasta* 17 who recorded at least 35 confirmed victories. In some ways his name is nearly synonymous with *Jasta* 17 – he served his entire career as a *Jagdflieger* within the *Staffel,* scoring its very first confirmed victory and finished the war as its commander.

Another 'Blue Max' recipient associated with the squadron's early period as *Kampfstaffel* Metz, conversely, became one of the most infamous figures of the 20th Century. Another of its most remarkable early pilots was perhaps not the most successful in terms of victories, but was certainly the *oldest* German fighter pilot of World War 1!

The aces of *Jasta* 17 served with distinction on a variety of fronts from the Metz region all the way to the North Sea. They flew with success against all comers, including amongst their opponents French, British, Belgian and American airmen. The *Jasta* achieved a proud record in exactly two years of frontline combat service, finishing the war with 101 confirmed victories.

The origins of *Jagdstaffel* 17 are closely linked to the historic and strategic fortress city of Metz, located at the confluence of the Moselle and the Seille Rivers in Lorraine. Today, Metz is a French city near the junction of France, Germany and Luxembourg, some 55 kilometres east of Verdun. The city, and its French fortifications, were annexed by the German Empire in 1871 as part of the Treaty of Frankfurt following the Franco-Prussian War. In this way Metz became a 'garrison city' of the Imperial German Army. The Germans strengthened and expanded the area's defences by constructing a series of forts and batteries from Mülhausen (today's Mulhouse, France) to Luxembourg.

As both heavier and lighter-than-air military aeronautics developed in the early years of the 20th century, the aerial aspects of defending the Metz region were not neglected. In 1909 it was decided to construct a base for Zeppelins of the German Army about eight kilometres south-southwest of Metz, between Augny and the Château de Frescaty. This would become known as Metz-Frescaty airfield, easily identified in many photographs due to its massive Zeppelin hangar and long row of permanent aeroplane hangars. In 1912 the field was further developed into a *Fliegerstation* (military aerodrome), and a training facility for future pilots of the burgeoning *Fliegertruppe* was established there.

Once mobilisation orders for the Great War were issued on 1 August 1914, it was intended that Metz, Strasbourg and other fortress cities were to be supplied with a *Festungs-Flieger-Abteilung* (a fortress or garrison flying unit) for reconnaissance purposes, as well as anti-aircraft batteries. The 2. *Festungs-Flieger-Abteilung* Metz was established on 17 November 1914 under the *Stabsoffizier der Flieger (Stofl* – Staff Officer for aviation within an Army) of the 5. *Armee.*

After a few months of operations the fortress flying units were proving to be of small value in their role of reconnaissance for the garrison towns. They were therefore re-equipped and absorbed into the army's *Feld* (field) formations with new designations. As a result, 2. *Festungs-Flieger-Abteilung* Metz was transformed into *Feld-Flieger-Abteilung* 71 (Field Flying Section 71) on 7 August 1915. It was this mobile two-seater reconnaissance section that would provide an initial nucleus of airmen for what would eventually become *Jasta* 17.

The introduction of the Fokker Eindecker in the summer of 1915 ushered in a new era in aerial warfare. At first the new fighters were attached singly to the *Feld-Flieger Abteilungen*, but eventually some units had as many as four monoplanes on strength. In 1916 these temporary groupings of fighters into small units for special operations became the norm. Such a formation might be designated as a *Kampfeinsitzer-Kommando* (single-seater fighter command, or *KEK*) or simply as a *Fokkerstaffel* or *Kampfstaffel*, but it generally remained attached to its parent two-seater *Abteilung*. FFA 71, still stationed at Metz, had received a few Fokker fighters by the summer of 1916 and soon formed its own *Kampfstaffel*.

KAMPFSTAFFEL METZ

Luckily for the researcher, a short history of *Jasta* 17 was composed at the end of the war by Buro-Uffz Karl Wasenmüller, the unit's NCO office clerk – it was published in the periodical *Deutsche Flugillustrierte* in 1935. According to Wasenmüller, on 4 July 1916 FFA 71 was transferred from Metz-Frescaty to Briey. However, a small detachment of two observation aircraft remained at Metz-Frescaty for use by the Metz military administration. Also assigned to Metz were two 100 hp Fokker E IIIs, a 160 hp Fokker E IV and a Halberstadt D-type fighter. The latter aircraft was an example of the generation of new biplane fighters that were starting to replace the Fokker monoplanes. These single-seaters were grouped into a fighter detachment for the defence of the Metz sector, which had been repeatedly targeted by French bombers.

Wasenmüller recorded that *Kampfstaffel* Metz was created on 23 July 1916 as a temporary unit within *Armee-Abteilung* C. Its commander was the veteran flier Hptm Kurt Schmickaly. Born in Berlin on 10 July 1888, Schmickaly was a pre-war pilot who had served in *Flieger-Bataillon* Nr 3 in 1914 and had flown in FFA 34. *Jasta* 17's top ace Julius Buckler wrote of Schmickaly, 'All old fliers know this name and mention it full of reverence. This outstanding flight officer was equally admirable as a superior and as a human being'.

Among the pilots who served in the oft-changing and fluid roster of men under Schmickaly's command were several destined for eventual fame as aces. These included 26-year-old Oblt Bruno Loerzer (later CO of *Jasta* 26 and then *Jagdgeschwader* III, and a 'Blue Max' ace with 44 victories) as well as his younger brother Gefr Fritz Loerzer, who would also lead *Staffel* 26 and gain a measure of his own notoriety with 11 confirmed victories. As many readers know, wherever one found Bruno Loerzer one usually found

The expansive Metz-Frescaty
aerodrome was the first base
of *Jasta* 17 and its ancestral
unit, *Kampfstaffel* Metz. Here,
Hptm Kurt Schmickaly, the first
commander of the *Kampfstaffel*,
tries out the rear cockpit of an
Albatros C V/16, possibly an aircraft
of FFA 71. Seen standing in front of
the aeroplane in the pullover sweater
is Bruno Loerzer, another early
member of the Metz *Kampfstaffel*.
The Zeppelin hangar that identified
the Metz-Frescaty field to all is just
out of frame to the left

his close friend and companion Hermann Göring as well – and this is true for this unit. The future leader of *Jasta* 27 and the final commander of the 'Richthofen *Jagdgeschwader*' (not to mention Luftwaffe commander and *Reichsmarschall* in the Nazi regime) gained some of his earliest experience as a fighter pilot in the Metz *Kampfstaffel* alongside Loerzer.

It is beyond the scope of this volume to cover the career of Hermann Göring in the Great War, or his later infamy. He was only briefly with *Kampfstaffel* Metz. Readers looking for such a detailed account should read Peter Kilduff's excellent and comprehensive recent work, *Hermann Göring, Fighter Ace – The World War I Career of Germany's Most Infamous Airman* (Grub Street, London, 2010). However, perhaps a brief recap of some the early experiences of the famous twosome of Göring and Loerzer up to their time in *Kampfstaffel* Metz is appropriate.

Göring went to war in August 1914 as an officer in the 4. *Badisches Infanterie-Regt 'Prinz Wilhelm'* Nr 112. It was in that unit that he met the man who would become a companion and early mentor, Bruno Loerzer. Born in Berlin-Friedenau on 22 January 1891, Loerzer was the first of the duo to become an aviator. He transferred from the regiment to the air service on 15 July 1914. Once the war began, Göring displayed considerable ability in early fighting near the Vosges Mountains, but in late September he was sidelined by acute rheumatoid arthritis in his knees and wound up in the Freiburg hospital.

Coincidentally, Bruno Loerzer was also in Freiburg at the Aviatik military flying school – he immediately visited his recuperating friend and suggested that Göring join him as his observer. After his recovery Göring did exactly that, securing a transfer for observer's training to *Flieger-Ersatz-Abteilung* 3 (an aviation training and replacement unit) in Darmstadt through bluster and guile.

Around the beginning of November 1914 both men were posted to FFA 25, attached to the 5. *Armee* at Stenay. There, the pair flew as a team for some months, earning the notice and patronage of their Army's commander, Crown Prince Wilhelm.

In July 1915 Göring was posted to the Aviatik Flying School for pilot's training, while Loerzer left for single-seater fighter school. Returning to FFA 25, Göring finally achieved his first undisputed victory when he and his observer were credited with a French Farman downed near Tahure on 16 November 1915.

By late June 1916, Oblt Loerzer had been assigned to fly one of the new Fokkers attached to FFA 25, while his friend sought out combat flying AEG G-type twin-engined aircraft and Albatros C III two-seaters. On 9 July, Göring achieved his cherished ambition of becoming a *Jagdflieger* when he was detached to *Artillerie-Flieger-Abteilung* 203 (artillery-spotting unit, abbreviated AFA 203) to fly a new Halberstadt D II 115/16. Loerzer continued to fly Eindecker fighters with FFA 25.

Both men were reunited on 23 July when they were assigned to fly Halberstadts from AFA 203 to the Metz sector to assist in its defence against French bombing raids. On 24 July Göring reported that his third flight of the day resulted in 'three aerial combats against Nieuports and two-seat Caudrons – both chased off'. Six days later, the ambitious Göring was credited with his third confirmed success when he brought down a twin-engined Caudron G 4 two-seater west of the Moselle.

On 5 August the pair of future aces returned to FFA 25, but about a month later both would report to the Metz *Kampfstaffel* to fly fighters under Schmickaly's command. Sources state that Göring was posted in on 6 or 9 September, while Bruno Loerzer may have appeared on the rolls of the unit as early as 23 July – his younger brother Fritz reported in from *KEK* Jametz on 14 August. At any rate, Bruno Loerzer and Göring are recorded as bringing two of the new Halberstadt D III biplanes (392/16 and 393/16) with them when they joined the Metz *Kampfstaffel*.

Oblt Stefan Kirmaier, who arrived on 30 August for a brief stay in *Kampfstaffel* Metz, was a veteran of *KEK* Jametz with three victories to his name already – he brought Halberstadt D II 109/16 with him. Born in Lachen, Bavaria, on 28 July 1889, Kirmaier had been wounded in the jaw at Verdun on 28 October 1914 whilst serving as a leutnant in the Bavarian *Infanterie-Regiment 'Grossherzog Friedrich II. Von Baden'* Nr 8. This necessitated almost two months' convalescence in a Metz hospital, followed by further time in Munich clinics until he was posted to a reserve infantry unit close to Metz on 11 September 1915. Kirmaier then commenced his flight training at the Bavarian facility at Schleissheim.

Following promotion to oberleutnant in January 1916, he was posted to *Kasta* 33 of *Kampfgeschwader* 6 on 1 April. His service there led to an assignment as an Eindecker exponent with the AFA 203 single-seater detachment, which would eventually be known as *KEK* Jametz. Kirmaier had destroyed two British aircraft and a balloon within two weeks of joining AFA 203, this success earning him a place as a charter member of the new autonomous fighter squadron *Jasta* 6 when it formed at Sivry on 25 August. As previously stated, he was soon loaned to *Kampfstaffel* Metz but only stayed with it until 8 September, when he returned to *Jasta* 6. This was followed by a move to Oswald Boelcke's own *Jasta* 2, where Kirmaier attained the balance of his 11 confirmed victories and was selected to command the unit after Boelcke's death on 28 October. On 22 November 1916 Kirmaier was killed in action dogfighting with DH 2 pushers from the Royal Flying Corps' No 24 Sqn.

Like Kirmaier, Göring and Bruno Loerzer saw little successful aerial combat during their brief sojourn in the Metz *Kampfstaffel*. In fact, the only action recorded during Göring's time there was when he had an inconclusive fight with two French *'Gitterrumpf'* machines near Nancy on 14 September. German airmen habitually used the terms *'Gitterrumpf'* ('lattice-fuselage') or *'Gitterschwanz'* ('lattice-tail') to refer to enemy pusher aeroplanes. These names were also applied to Caudron G 3 and G 4 tractor-engined machines, as they had openwork twin tail booms. Göring was transferred to *Jasta* 7 at Martincourt-sur-Meuse on 21 or 28 September, and Bruno Loerzer would leave the Metz *Kampfstaffel* at about the same time.

A few examples of Halberstadt D II and D III fighters were posted to *Kampfstaffel* Metz. Although this particular D II was not assigned to the unit, its pilot is Hermann Göring, who briefly flew with the Metz *Staffel* in September 1916 (*J Young*)

Two other future stalwarts who served – albeit only briefly – with *Kampfstaffel Metz* were Vzfw Hans Imelmann and Ltn Joachim von Bertrab. Young Imelmann (no relation to the celebrated ace Max Immelmann) chalked up six confirmed victories as an early member of Boelcke's *Jasta* before he was killed on 23 January 1917. Joachim von Bertrab went on to gain five victories in *Jasta* 30 before his attempt to flame a balloon near Souchez on 12 August 1917 ended with him being shot down by ace Edward 'Mick' Mannock of No 40 Sqn and captured. Ltn von Bertrab survived the war, but died at the age of just 27 in 1922.

JAKOB WOLFF

Of all the men who achieved a measure of success in *Kampfstaffel* Metz, as well as *Jasta* 17, one stands out for several remarkable reasons. Unfortunately, Jakob Wolff remains relatively unknown to most World War 1 aviation enthusiasts today. Although he just missed reaching ace status by modern standards with 'only' four undisputed victories (and several unconfirmed claims), the obstacles he overcame make his story an important one.

Before the war Wolff was an avowed pacifist who contributed significant funds to that cause. Furthermore, as a wealthy industrialist whose factory employed thousands of workers he was certainly exempt from military service. Then there was the small matter of his age. By the time of his final victory, Wolff was 48 years old, making him the oldest fighter pilot in the entire army of Imperial Germany, if not all the warring nations. But beyond those barriers, there was one more – Wolff was a Jew.

Jakob Johannes Wolff was born in Hamburg on 21 March 1869. His father Louis had risen from humble origins to establish the eminently successful cigar factory 'L Wolff' in Hamburg (with a branch in Hessisch-Lichenau), which employed some 4000 workers. By October 1890 Jakob was fulfilling his military service obligation as a member of the Bavarian 11. *Infanterie-Regiment von der Tann* in Regensburg. He attempted to become an officer of the reserves but was unsuccessful, being advised that in order to secure promotion he would have to renounce his Jewish faith and be baptised a Christian. Wolff considered himself a 'free thinker' and was not particularly devout in his approach to Judaism. Indeed, in 1912 he left the synagogue association, but he did not abandon the Jewish faith or other Jewish organisations. Nevertheless, he rejected the recommendation that he be baptised merely to become an officer as hypocritical.

At some point Jakob took over his father's factory and used his wealth to promote the pacifist movement for a period of 28 years – he donated 45,000 *Reichsmarks* to anti-war causes. Nevertheless, when the Great War erupted his patriotic fervour and a deep sense of duty overrode his pacifist leanings. On 2 August 1914 Jakob presented himself to the Hamburg district command as a 45-year-old volunteer. His application was quickly – and contemptuously – dismissed, but that did not stop a man of Wolff's determination.

Flying had already seized his imagination, so he paid for private flying lessons and purchased his own aeroplane. He duly presented himself and his machine at the *Flieger-Ersatz-Abteilung* (FEA) 2 at Adlershof, in Berlin, and announced that he was ready to serve to the nonplussed authorities. He again received a frosty reception, being told to return to Hamburg. While there had not been any age limit specified for German military pilots, Wolff was told that he was far too old. No doubt his Jewish ancestry played a part as well, for there was considerable anti-Semitism in the German officer corps in 1914.

Vzfw Wolff persisted, however, and finally a 'kind though senile superior who had no concept of flying' allowed him to stay on. He was accepted for training as a military airman and made 60 solo flights during his tenure at FEA 1. On 23 November 1915 Vzfw Wolff was assigned to *Kampfeinsitzer-Abteilung* 1 at Mannheim, where he was again met with incredulity and obstruction. He was informed that he was too old to handle a single-seater, and (falsely) informed that only officers could fly fighters. Summarily rejected, he was packed off to *Armee-Flug-Park* (AFP) 5 (an aviation supply depot).

The circumstances are not fully known, but somehow Wolff managed to get himself posted to FFA 34 at Cunel as a Fokker pilot – he finally made his first flight as a frontline combatant on 31 January 1916. On that mission he was operating as a *Sperrflieger* (barrier or blockade pilot), and due to his inexperience he became disoriented. After landing near a village to get his bearings, Wolff safely returned to Cunel. Unfortunately, a few days later he again became lost on a flight after engaging a French Farman. This second instance of losing his way was sufficient to get Wolff sacked. As he was ignominiously returning to the rear in a truck on 8 March, he saw his erstwhile comrades flying overhead. 'I could no longer bear it. For an hour I sat broken and stared ahead fixedly'.

Wolff's resilient character came through, however, and he later managed a posting to FFA 71 at Metz-Frescaty on 18 June. He distinguished himself there by test-flying aircraft. During one hot summer's day at Metz, Wolff was among those watching various soldiers take a swim in a local watering hole. A certain Obgefr Lenz suffered a cramp and disappeared beneath the surface. No one bestirred themselves except the 'old man' from Hamburg. Wolff saved the soldier from drowning and earned the praise of the governor of Metz, Adolf von Oven, in the official order of 20 June (as well as the German Lifesaving Medal).

As a direct result of this incident, Kurt Schmickaly agreed to Wolff's transfer to his *Kampstaffel* on 23 July. The cigar manufacturer's career as a *Jagdflieger* finally took off. Although he still occasionally experienced some anti-Semitic remarks from his fellow pilots, Wolff seems to have been generally respected by his comrades. He wrote in his diary, 'But I must insert here now that Schmickaly is very fair. He sees things only from a flier's perspective'.

For some time French aircraft of the 1st and 2nd *Groupes de Bombardement* had targeted the railway station and barracks at Metz by frequent bombing raids, and it was the primary duty of *Kampstaffel* Metz to try to obstruct such attacks. On 22 July, for instance, the Caudrons of *Escadrille* C66 had carried out three successive missions against the Metz-Sablon railway station. The contemporary French bombing historian René Martel wrote that 'for those familiar with the anti-aircraft defences of Metz and the unforgiving viciousness of the squadrons from nearby Frescaty, the triple expedition of 22 July seemed like an extraordinary act of courage'.

Wolff was doing his part (most likely in a Fokker monoplane) to defend Metz, and on 16 August he shot down a Caudron *'Gitterschwanz'* over NoMény. The necessary witnesses, however, were not forthcoming, and he failed to obtain confirmation. In spite of this he received the grateful thanks of the General Officer in charge of the Metz sector, *Exzellenz* von Hoffmeister, in person.

It was said that for a week after 2 September Wolff was almost a one-man *Kampfstaffel,* responsible for the entire defence of the region due to illnesses and transfers of his fellow pilots. Finally, this resulted in the award of his Pilot's Badge (a significant milestone for any frontline pilot) on 10 September 1916, eight months after his first combat flight. Wolff subsequently became a well-respected member of the *Kampfstaffel,* befriending Bruno Loerzer and others.

The Fokker Eindecker revolutionised aerial warfare. This is a Fokker E III of *Kampfstaffel* Metz, with Vzfw Jakob Wolff in the cockpit. The *Kampfstaffel* was originally a temporary detachment of single-seat fighters attached to FFA 71. At 47 years of age, Wolff was the oldest fighter pilot in the German air service (*N W O'Connor*)

This close-up of Jakob Wolff in his Fokker E III shows that he sported a moustache for a time, but it is gone in later photographs. The serial number of Wolff's Fokker is unknown, but it seems to have come from the 601-636/15 batch. Wolff claimed to have shot down a Caudron in this aeroplane on 16 August 1916 but its demise was not confirmed (*N W O'Connor*)

The *Kampfstaffel* Metz pilots assembled for a group photograph, *circa* September 1916. They are, from left to right, Vzfw Jakob Wolff, Vzfw Eduard Ey, Offz Stv Neumann, Ltn Hermann Göring, unknown, Oblt Stefan Kirmaier, Hptm Kurt Schmickaly (the unit CO, with cigar), Ltn Georg Zeumer and Offz Stv Kern. Zeumer is famous for having been Manfred von Richthofen's pilot when the latter flew as an observer in FFA 69. It is not known if Zeumer was actually a member of *KEK* Metz at this time or was merely a visitor (*P Kilduff*)

FORMATION OF *JAGDSTAFFEL* 17

It was during this period that momentous events overtook Wolff and the others of *Kampfstaffel* Metz, as *Jasta* 17's chronicler Karl Wasenmüller recalled;

'Day and night French bomber squadrons penetrated the Front and extensively carpeted the areas of Metz, the Sablon railway station and the industrial area near Hagendingen with bombs. Aerial protection, therefore, had to be strengthened. Upon repeated petitions by the Governor of the *Festung* Metz, *AOK* 5 [the Army Headquarters of the 5. *Armee*] admitted to *Stofl* 5 and the *Feldflugchef* that the aerial protection of Metz was definitely insufficient. After all, combat aircraft had been retained to protect other cities of only indirect military significance in the interior [such as Trier and Cologne, which were only rarely or never attacked by enemy aircraft], while – during good flying weather – the *Festung* Metz, standing so near the enemy, was attacked daily.

'It was proposed by the Governor of Metz, von Oven, that half a *Jagdstaffel* would be transferred to Metz. The 5. *Armee* was, at that time, in possession of only seven single-seater fighter aircraft to oppose the French combat aeroplanes. Because the creation of a *Jagdstaffel* was, by all means, supported, Metz was allocated a *Jagdstaffel* on 11 November 1916, and this was in fact the current *Jagdstaffel* 17.'

According to official sources, *Jasta* 17 was created on 23 October 1916 in accordance with the order *Kommandierer General der Luftstreitkräfte von 23-10-16 Nr 26665 Fl*. It was recorded as operational on Metz-Frescaty airfield on 11 November 1916 – exactly two years before the armistice. The unit was largely formed from the nucleus of *Kampfstaffel* Metz, and it drew the remainder of its personnel from AFP 5. Among those pilots who transferred directly from the *Kampfstaffel* to the new *Jasta* 17 were Vzfw Jakob Wolff, Ltn d R Wilhelm Gros, Offz Stv Neumann, Ltn d R Robert Lessing and Offz Stv Kern. Hptm Kurt Schmickaly had been logically scheduled to serve as the first commander of the new *Jagdstaffel*, but on 22 October he was severely wounded in the stomach during a combat over Malzeville, near Nancy. He died of his wounds the next day, just as *Jasta* 17 was born.

The leadership of the new *Staffel* was therefore passed to nobleman *Rittmeister* Anton Heinz *Freiherr* von Brederlow, who transferred in from *Kampfstaffel* 21 of *Kagohl* 4 on 11 November 1916. Wasenmüller wrote;

'The *Staffel* was assembled on Frescaty airfield, the former *Fliegerstation* Metz, as a field aviation unit of the 5. *Armee*. The task of the *Staffel* was the aerial protection of Metz and the nearby industrial area, and to attack squadrons breaking though into the homeland. Newly-created *Jagdstaffel* 17, utilising all of its available resources, fulfilled these first duties in an exemplary fashion.'

Wasenmüller wrote that *Jasta* 17 was equipped with the Albatros D II, but his recollection was a bit optimistic. The D II was Germany's newest and best fighter, fitted with the powerful 160 hp Mercedes D III engine and armed with twin Maxim lMG 08/15 machine guns. While *Jasta* 17 initiated its existence with at least *some* Albatros D IIs, it seems the unit was only partially equipped with the new type, and still retained some Fokker E III and twin-gun E IV machines, as well as some Halberstadt D-types.

Jakob Wolff perches on the cockpit rim of a well-used Eindecker. The machine gun seen here featured a different sighting device than the one seen in the other photographs of Wolff's Fokker. Wolff was one of those who transferred from *Kampfstaffel* Metz to the newly formed *Jasta* 17 upon its formation

The flight log of Georg Strasser, another charter member of the *Jasta* and one of its eventual greats, still exists and sheds some light on the early equipment of the *Staffel*. On 14 and 16 November he recorded flights in Halberstadts, but on the 21st he flew a 100 hp Fokker (probably an E III) and six days later a 160 hp Fokker E IV. On 27 November he logged time on a 100 hp Fokker and made a test flight in Albatros D II 1712/16. As time went on, more of the highly desired Albatros fighters arrived, yet Strasser recorded a flight in a 100 hp Fokker as late as 12 December 1916. In an undated incident from this period, Jakob Wolff is said to have downed another unconfirmed Caudron – which was nevertheless deemed worthy of the personal appreciation of Gen von Oven.

This fine view of three distinctly marked D II fighters on Metz-Frescaty airfield reveals 520/16 in the foreground. It displays an 'Iron Cross ribbon' as a personal marking, most likely in Prussian black and white colours. Next is 502/16, which would also later be flown by Georg Strasser on a patrol from St Quentin-le-Petit on 11 March 1917. Last in line is an OAW-built D II, possibly 927/16 – note how the fuselage cross on OAW products was painted in a forward position

Julius Buckler was a charter member of *Jasta* 17, and no one else would be more associated with the unit, or attain more victories for it. This photograph shows him after he had been made an officer and had been awarded the *Pour le Mérite* in December 1917 (*N W O'Connor*)

As noted, Vzfw Julius Buckler was with the *Jagdstaffel* from its formation, and he would fly with the unit for two years and emerge as its top ace. In 1939 Buckler wrote or dictated an anecdotal account of his war years entitled *'Malaula!' Der Kampfruf meiner Staffel* ('*Malaula!* The Battle-cry of My Squadron'). It was a popular book in its day, and its 'ripping yarns' style of storytelling still makes for exciting reading. However, *'Malaula!'* is basically an oral history, and poor history at that. It is a collection of an old pilot's tales, recounted without reference to official records. It gives us an evocative glimpse of the character of its author, but it provides few dates (when it does, they are often in error) or hard reliable facts. Nevertheless, some insights can be gleaned from this work, as ably translated by Adam Wait and edited by Norman Franks, and kindly quoted with their permission.

Buckler was born on 28 March 1894 in the Hessian city of Mainz, on the Rhine. Buckler's father was a roofer, and Buckler made much of his humble working-class origins in his book. In the winters a roofer's job opportunities dried up, so Buckler's mother washed clothes to help out – young Buckler and his two sisters hardly noticed the hard times. As a student Buckler was not exactly a great scholar, and he started work as a roofer's apprentice at the age of 12. According to Walter Zuerl's book *Pour le Mérite Flieger,* in 1909 the young Hessian got his first taste of aviation when he briefly met Anthony Fokker, who was working with Jacob Goedecker in building aircraft and attending an engineering school in Zahlbach. Buckler wrote that he occasionally helped Fokker by 'washing out benzene cans', and that he was taken on a very short test hop as a reward.

On 15 October 1912 the 18-year-old joined the 8th Company of the Hessian Grand Ducal Division's *Infanterie-Leibregiment Grossherzogin (3. Hessisches) Nr 117,* and it was with this unit that he went to war as an unteroffizier less than two years later.

Buckler picked up the first of his many wounds in September 1914 as his regiment was engaged in the fighting on the Marne. He had already received the Iron Cross 2nd Class in August, but in hand-to-hand combat he suffered a broken left shoulder and a wound to the knee. After his recovery he was declared 'fit for garrison duty' only, so he began submitting petitions for a transfer to the air service. At the end of November his persistence was rewarded with a transfer to FEA 6 in Grossenhain, Saxony, for pilot training. He moved on to the DFW flight school in Leipzig-Lindenthal in December, and passed the field pilot's examination after only four weeks – earning him an extra four-week leave. However, when he returned he was disappointed to discover he had been made an instructor.

Buckler's long-desired return to the front came in the summer of 1915 when he joined *Artillerie-Flieger-Abteilung* 209 under the command of Hptm Werner Funck. It was there that Buckler formed a deep friendship and working relationship with his observer Oblt Kurt Hubertus *Freiherr* von Rudno-Rudzinski. The two became so close during their months of ranging the big guns on such targets as Forts Vaux and Douaumont that 'Rudno' would eventually follow Buckler to *Jasta* 17 after he gained his pilot's license.

On 21 March 1916, Buckler (with 'Rudno' as observer) dived his two-seater at a French Voisin with the intention of attacking it, when out of nowhere a Fokker Eindecker intervened in the fight and shot down the 'pusher' right under their noses. The Fokker pilot then landed at the aerodrome of AFA 209, climbed out and introduced himself as 'Boelcke'. The great ace had just attained his 13th victory, and this meeting left Buckler with a burning desire to become a *Jagdflieger*.

That desire was finally met when Buckler received a telegram asking him if he would care to join the new *Staffel* 17. 'On 11 November 1916 I reported to the commanding officer of the newly formed *Jasta* 17, *Rittm* von Brederlow, on the big Metz airfield at Frescaty', wrote Buckler. 'The good Schmickaly was already dead'.

The aforementioned Georg Strasser was another founding member of the *Jasta*. Strasser was born on 10 November 1891 in Leukerstetten, in the Kingdom of Württemberg. One of four children of a postman, he manifested an interest in mechanics and the new technologies at an early age. During his studies as an artist in Stuttgart, the 20-year-old befriended a like-minded mechanic named August Ströbel. The two collaborated on building a primitive monoplane with a 50 hp Antoinette engine. Young Strasser bravely chose to pilot the machine, and on 24 August 1912 he made a two-minute flight up to an altitude of 30 metres.

However, the brave new world of aviation did not appeal to everyone, and after the flight Strasser's father was contacted by the *Bürgermeister* of Stuttgart and called to account for his son's action (Georg was still legally a minor). The elder Strasser was fined for his son's 'disturbance of the public order'. The sting of this punishment was alleviated somewhat when the local magistrate announced he would pay half the fine – the residents of Stuttgart were still proud of their local boys' enterprise. The two young inventors persisted, making two additional flights on 31 December, having switched out their first motor for a 90 hp Anzani. During the machine's 12th flight, made on 13 May 1913, Strasser crashed badly, wrecking the monoplane and receiving slight injuries.

When the war began the 22-year-old Württemberger naturally opted for the air service, and succeeded in getting assigned to *Fliegerbataillon* 4 in Freiburg im Breisgau. Strasser completed his training in Freiburg and went on to the military *Fliegerschule* in Gotha on 13 September 1915. Promoted to unteroffizier, he continued his pilot training at FEA 3, and made his first solo flight only nine days before his 24th birthday. In spite of the winter weather, his drive to succeed continued, and he completed his schooling in Gotha on 26 January 1916. Strasser attained more experience at the Metz *Fliegerschule* and was then posted to AFP 5 at Montmédy on 12 April, being judged fit for assignment to a frontline unit by 6 May 1916. He was soon posted to FFA 44, and carried out many photographic missions in Albatros C III 4063/15.

On 4 August he was flying with an Oblt Lindenberg in Albatros C III 787/16 when the two faced off against a Farman near Fleury – the French crew managed to escape. On 10 September Strasser's Albatros was attacked by two twin-engined Caudron G 4s, the German claiming to have shot one down. Indeed, he described its fall with precision, stating the aircraft fell one kilometre south of Gremilly. However, a counter-claim was made by a flak battery and Strasser angrily recorded in his logbook that the Caudron was not granted to him.

Georg Strasser was another outstanding charter member of *Staffel* 17. He flew this Albatros D II 1712/16 from late November 1916 through to February 1917. It was marked with a black '3' on the fuselage and black(?) and white stripes. The stripe patterns and numbers probably identified different *Ketten* (flights) within *Jasta* 17, but their precise significance is not fully understood. The Zeppelin hangar of the Metz-Frescaty aerodrome looms in the background

He was mollified somewhat when he was rewarded for his aggressive tactics with a posting to *Jasta* 17. Now, like Buckler, Strasser had achieved his ambition of becoming an *Einsitzer* (single-seater) pilot. Buckler wrote, 'At least one flew alone, had two machine guns – and was a *Jagdflieger*'.

On 14 November Strasser made a test flight from Metz in a Halberstadt D-type, and on the 15th he led a patrol at 4000 metres over the Pont-à-Mousson sector. On 17 November his logbook recorded two sorties in Halberstadt D II 115/16. Of the first mission, he wrote, 'Over Pont-à-Mousson, a fight with Nieuport and Caudron at 3000 metres'. On the second flight of that day (lasting 132 minutes) he had another inconclusive engagement with a Nieuport fighter. According to Wasenmüller's records, in November 1916 the airmen of *Jasta* 17 logged 70 flights for a total of 57.75 flying hours and engaged in seven aerial combats. Despite their best efforts not a single confirmed victory had been achieved.

Even without any confirmed combat successes, former infantrymen like Buckler could appreciate the comfortable amenities of life in a *Staffel* situated close to a major German city. 'The weather alternated between rain and fog', Buckler wrote. 'At least this time I did not live, as I had a year before, in a cold corrugated tin barracks with rats and mice. I had a splendid room with central heating and running water. For the trip to the airfield at Metz we only needed a few minutes, and of course, money. We therefore arranged it so that twice a week we went out in style – that is, in Metz – and three times a week we stayed in Montigny, a village in the vicinity. There, we sat in the "House of the Three Maids". Thus we led wonderful and carefree lives'.

FIRST VICTORIES

Carefree they may have been, but the pilots of *Jasta* 17 still had their missions to fulfill – even as December brought declining flight conditions. In the last month of 1916 the *Staffel* pilots recorded 112 front flights for a total of 130.5 hours flying time, and took part in 15 aerial combats. However, few had much experience in aerial combat, and it was a steep learning curve for all. With his usual self-deprecating humour, Buckler recalled, 'In the time from 11 November up to 24 December 1916, I imagined that I'd fought the most ferocious air combats ever because I was using the most ammunition in the *Staffel*. At this time, I was using both machine gun belts on every fighter patrol but without any success!'

17

It was in one of these 'ferocious air combats', however, that Buckler achieved the honour of claiming *Jasta* 17's first undisputed aerial victory on 17 December;

'It was a winter day like any other when I took off in clear weather in a new machine, an Albatros D II, in order – driven by my demon – to scout the sky for the enemy, of whom I dreamt day and night. The sky was a bright empty grey expanse, a poor game preserve for a young, hot-blooded hunter. Damn, I thought, up here the sky is one big hunting ground – there are no borders and no hunting licenses. I pushed the engine wide open.

'Below me lay Verdun. My old comrades [of AFA 209] were quartered not far from here. I wondered whether any of them might meet me. Then about 200 metres below me I saw one of the observation aircraft of my old *Abteilung* crabbing around, but at the same time I spotted directly over Fort Douaumont yet another aircraft – in fact, a *"Gitterschwanz"*! Without much deliberation I put my machine on its nose and raced past the observation aircraft into the depths below. How I did not ram the Farman (sic) remains a mystery. I sped past him too.

'Missed! What was the meaning of this? I really was a fool. I tore the machine around on its wingtips, and now began the game of turning. The lattice-tail was slower than I, but the French aviator was by far the better pilot. His observer greeted me with a couple of decent bursts from his machine gun. What a laughable novice I was. In my time there were still no schools for fighter pilots, there was not even re-training for those going into fighter aircraft. One was merely put in his crate and then it was "off you go". Everyone had to gain his own experience.

'Umpteen times I sped past the Farman and fired for all I was worth. Finally I noticed that the observer was no longer to be seen. Where was he? Was he hiding, wounded or dead? Then I saw that the *"Gitterschwanz"* aircraft tilted and began to spin. I stuck doggedly behind him. A cloud of dust – the aircraft burst apart and was scattered in pieces.

'Soaked to the skin from excitement, I sped above the ground, and then I saw Azannes lying beneath me. It was my first aerial victory, yet I could not be glad about it. Now, after it was all over, I thought only of the two brave fellows who now lay on the hill, dead or with broken, mutilated limbs. I thought of their parents and brothers and sisters.'

If Buckler did indeed have such remorseful, compassionate thoughts at the time, it would have been quite unique for a young pilot who had just achieved his first *Luftsieg*. Indeed, he was still worried enough about getting his success confirmed that he landed at the familiar airfield of his old AFA 209;

'Although it was already afternoon, Hptm Funck, who greeted me warmly, had another aeroplane takeoff which snapped an aerial photograph of the wreckage of the lattice-tail aircraft. With the congratulations of my comrades, with "Schnurps", the dog given to me as a present, and with eggs and butter on board, I took off again and flew back to the *Staffel*.'

Ltn d R Heinz Sachsenberg, seen here at Metz-Frescaty, was posted to *Jasta* 17 from AFP 1 on 9 December 1916. Apparently, he was not closely related to his namesake Gotthard, the famous naval ace. Heinz Sachsenberg was an example of those steady comrades of such stars as Buckler and Strasser who provided support on patrols but failed to tally any victories themselves

In spite of Buckler's detailed description, it has proven difficult to corroborate this victory with French accounts. This first victory for *Jasta* 17 was timed at 1620 hrs (unless otherwise specified, all times noted in this book are German time, which was often one hour ahead of Allied time) and placed south of Bras in German records. It may have in fact been a twin-engined Caudron G 4 and not a 'Farman'. The only possible corresponding loss in the sparse French records is Sgt Raymond Choisnet of *Escadrille* C74, who was merely recorded as injured.

During this same period Buckler's friend Strasser was making frequent flights in Albatros D II 1712/16, a machine he had first flown on 27 November and which he would use almost exclusively until mid-February 1917. In an odd anomaly, Strasser's flight log record that he too scored his first confirmed *Luftsieg* on 17 December, the same day as Buckler's success. However, official records clearly state that Strasser's first victory did not come until Christmas Eve, when he was credited with a Caudron at 1640 hrs northwest of Fort Douaumont. This is believed to have been a machine of *Escadrille* C34 that fell in flames northwest of Douaumont at Aspach on 24 December – the crew of MdL Jean Hourcade and Sous Lt Lombart both perished.

Strasser's own record of a claimed victory on 17 December is still noteworthy. On just his 14th flight as a fighter pilot, he took off in D II 1712/16 toward Verdun;

'North of Douaumont a hellish artillery fire and about six Caudrons flying infantry cooperation patrol at 200 metres height. Attacked one of them from behind. After 300 rounds he crashed among the shell holes. Return flight through barrage fire at 50 to 100 metres height. Landed at Metz at onset of darkness.'

If Strasser's first victory actually did come on 24 December (as official records have it) and not the 17th, his *Flugbuch* does not record it. On the 21st he flew D II 1712/16 on a *Jagdflug* (fighter patrol) at an altitude of 2000 metres, but rain and stormy weather forced him to land at the airfield of his old *Abteilung* 44. On Christmas Eve he participated in a *Geschwader-Jagdflug* (a flight in full squadron strength) for 95 minutes at 3500 metres – yet still with no combat reported in his flight log.

However, a mission flown the previous day was eventful for Buckler. Many years later he wrote;

'The 23rd of December 1916 gave me my first enlightenment as to what "being a *Jagdflieger*" means. On that day, I experienced the strangest thing you can imagine. Over Fort Vaux, I was unexpectedly attacked by three Nieuports and, under constant fire, was accompanied by these three fellows as far as my own airfield. The really lucky part of the whole thing was that these three Frenchmen were stupid beginners, just as I was. And this fight was a signal for me – "Open your eyes, pay attention, become a fighter pilot".'

The following day Buckler apparently received the supreme Christmas present of the *Ehrenbecher*, the prestigious silver 'honour cup' which was presented to German airmen in recognition of their initial victory – in this case Buckler's 'kill' of 17 December.

It is believed that Buckler's next adventure occurred on 26 December, although in his book he erroneously ascribes it to Christmas Day. With the temperature standing at 17 degrees below freezing, Buckler wrapped himself up and had his guns loaded with incendiary ammuniter. He now planned to try his hand at 'sausage burning', since a French balloon had conspicuously hung in the area of Pont-à-Mousson for the previous three weeks. Buckler took off in his Albatros D II christened *Mops* (which loosely translates as 'Pug'), climbed to altitude and flew about 20 kilometres in the direction of the enemy. He then turned to attack the 'gasbag', as he subsequently explained to author Walter Zuerl;

Ltn d R Wilhelm Gros is seen in the cockpit of his Albatros D II 1727/16 '1' as an unidentified comrade stands nearby. In the winter of 1916-17, Gros was the first pilot in the *Staffel* to perform a loop, inspiring his friends Strasser and Buckler to emulate his feat of airmanship

'My machine guns were chattering, and I looked toward the balloon, which was still refusing to burn. My machine guns continued to chatter – they weren't jammed, but my ammunition was gone. All this played out in such a short time, and I was so preoccupied with my nerves that it was only upon nearing the balloon that I first realised just how large a captive balloon actually is. My fright was so great that I very nearly ran right into the balloon at full speed. My fear was heightened when I heard terrible machine gun fire behind me. Moreover, my propeller suddenly stopped. I had to proceed to land like a glider pilot, setting *Mops* down on unfamiliar terrain heavily covered with snow, but which fortunately was smooth.'

Buckler related the same tale in *'Malaula!'*, with some of the usual discrepancies. He stated that soon after he landed near Mailly, French artillery targeted the area and he rapidly exited the Albatros to take cover in a shell hole. The D II received a direct hit and he was forced to return to the *Staffel* on foot.

In addition to Buckler, Strasser and Wolff, another distinguished charter member of *Jasta* 17 who enters the story here is Ltn d R Wilhelm Emmanuel Gros. Born in Karlsruhe (the capital of Baden) on 6 July 1892, Gros was studying mechanical engineering when World War 1 commenced. He duly enlisted at the *Kraftwagen-Depot* (motor vehicle depot) in Frankfurt am Main on 19 October 1914. Following a brief stay at *Etappen-Kraftwagen-Park 2*, Gros was assigned to FFA 27 in the Verdun sector in January 1915 as a mechanical specialist.

He desired a more active role, however, and on 1 June Gros was sent to FEA 5 at Hannover to initiate his flight training. He attended the *Militär-Flieger-Schule* in Halberstadt from 19 June to 23 August, and then finished his training back at FEA 5. Promoted to unteroffizier on 18 September, Gros was posted to FAA 207 on the Champagne Front about five weeks later. Rising quickly, he qualified for his *Flugzeugführer-Abzeichen* (pilot's badge) on 11 January 1916 and earned promotion to vizefeldwebel on 13 April, having already received the Iron Cross 2nd Class. Gros was awarded Baden's Silver Military Medal on 10 June 1916 and promoted to leutnant in the reserves on 28 September. The EK I (Iron Cross 1st Class) inevitably followed on 11 October. Gros was appointed to *Jasta* 17 upon its formation, having first served briefly in *Kampfstaffel* Metz.

It was during the long periods of inactivity in the winter of 1916-17 that Gros, Strasser and Buckler devised a unique way to pass the time. While most of the pilots whiled away the hours drinking, reading, playing chess or card games, these three 'die-hards' who could not get enough of flying sat in a corner and discussed aerobatics. At this time, the average German military pilot had little experience with 'trick flying', which was not actively taught in the schools. Most frontline airmen had never looped and did not know how to recover from a spin. Buckler wrote that the three die-hards practiced their proposed aerobatics with paper aeroplanes and heated discussion.

On one such day, the weather cleared up enough for Ltn d R Gros to obtain permission for a flight. Suddenly his Albatros roared over the pilots' mess, and everyone rushed out just in time to witness Gros executing a 'genuine loop' just like the famous French pre-war airman Pégoud – *'Donnerwetter!'* Now getting the hang of it, Gros described one loop after another. Buckler noticed that Strasser, too, had taken to his Albatros and after his fourth try succeeded in completing the same manoeuvre. Emboldened, Buckler rose to the challenge and had his *Mops* No 2 prepared. After a number of failed attempts he succeeded in emulating Gros and Strasser. Soon Buckler was astonished to see a 'regular circus' above the Metz-Frescaty airfield as the entire *Staffel* was now in the air attempting loops.

According to Buckler, that evening (20 December 1916 apparently, as Strasser's *Flugbuch* makes reference to 'two loops' on that day) the pilots hatched a risky plan to impress their girlfriends in Metz the next day. Sure enough, the following morning, the incredulous citizens of Metz witnessed a 'mating dance in the sky' as the impetuous young pilots 'serenaded' their lady friends with a show of trick flying. The higher authorities were, Buckler said, not exactly amused.

1917

As 1916 gave way to 1917 some new names began to achieve notoriety within the *Staffel*, while other familiar ones attained new successes and some moved on to adventures elsewhere. Ltn d R Günther Schuster had been posted in from FEA 7 on 23 December 1916. An accomplished musician and skilled horseman, the future ace Schuster would serve two separate tours of duty with *Jasta* 17 and rise to command the *Staffel* in June 1918.

Vzfw Rieger was, like Buckler, Strasser and Gros, a charter member of *Jagdstaffel* 17, having previously served in FFA 1. While he failed to achieve a large number of victories, he would claim at least two, one of which remained unconfirmed by the strict standards of the *Fliegertruppe*. In the caption to an original album photograph of Rieger in the author's possession, the bespectacled airman is described as having 'four enemy aircraft *abgeschossen*' (sic), so he was considered highly successful in the eyes of at least some of his contemporaries.

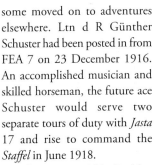

A happy Vzfw Rieger is seen in the cockpit of Albatros D II '1' (possibly 518/16) at Metz. The original album caption for this photograph stated that Rieger had shot down four enemy aircraft. He may have *claimed* that many, but only one was apparently confirmed

One ace-to-be who passed briefly through *Jasta* 17's roster was Vzfw Fritz John Jacobsen. Born on 7 July 1894 in Berlin-Charlottenberg, as a two-year-old he witnessed some of the flights of gliding pioneer Otto Lilienthal. 'Jac' Jacobsen attained his civilian pilot's license at the age of 20 in July 1914. He then joined the *Fliegertruppe* and received military flight training at FEA 3. By March 1915 he had earned his Pilot's Badge. The following June Jacobsen was assigned to FFA 1 and flew in campaigns in Galicia, Serbia and Macedonia. A transfer to the Western Front in May 1916 brought him the opportunity to volunteer for fighter pilot training, and he went to the *Kampf-Einsitzer-Schule* in Mannheim-Sandhofen. During service with *Kampf-Einsitzer-Abteilung* 1 he participated in an attack on French bombers raiding Karlsruhe, but crashed in flames.

Following recuperation Jacobsen was assigned to AFP 5 at Autrécourt until his posting to *Jasta* 17 on 11 November 1916. He did not stay long, transferring to *Jasta* 9 in December, but soon switched units again, this time to *Jasta* 31 on the 15th of that month. Jacobsen attained his first *Luftsieg* on 6 July, and his second on 19 August. He travelled to Italy with *Jasta* 31 in September, making two unconfirmed claims on that Front. Jacobsen joined *Jasta* 73 back on the Western Front in March 1918, where he would score six more victories. Having survived the war, he died in 1981 at the age of 87.

Other *Jasta* 17 airmen did their best to continue their active defence of the Metz area in January 1917, but the poor flying weather limited their actions. That month the unit logged 81 flights for a total of 84.75 hours in the air. Fifteen aerial combats were experienced, but January was nearly out before one of these reached a successful conclusion. On 29 January Ltn d R Günther Schuster was credited with a Caudron destroyed at Nomény for his first victory, and the third for his *Jagdstaffel*. The following day the *Staffel* welcomed new pilot Ltn Alfred Träger, a cheerful flier with previous service in KG 4. He would remain a popular and reliable, if not outstanding, member of the *Staffel* until June 1918.

Meanwhile, misfortune had continued to follow the efforts of the indefatigable Vzfw Jakob Wolff, who was now approaching his 48th birthday. Flying an Albatros D II, he attacked a Voisin 'pusher' on 2 February 1917 and forced it down to the earth south of Regineville. However, he was once again denied credit for an official victory, instead being merely cited with a zLgzw claim for *zur Landung gezwungen* (forced to land in Allied territory). While this entered his name in the official *Jasta* record book, it did not count as a full victory. His score remained at zero. Six days later he crashed into some trees (probably in OAW-built Albatros D II 933/16) but survived unhurt.

John Fritz Jacobsen seems to have taken D II 518/16 with him when he left *Jasta* 17 in December 1916. After a very brief stint with *Jasta* 9 he went to *Jasta* 31, where this photograph was taken. On the left is D II 518/16, still bearing its *Jasta* 17 markings of a zigzag band and number '1'. On the right is Jacobsen's new Albatros D III 2090/16, with the diamond band marking he used in *Jasta* 31. Jacobsen is apparently the man on the right

Ltn d R Günther Schuster joined *Jasta* 17 on 23 December 1916 and attained his first victory on 29 January 1917. He is seen here at the end of the war, after he had achieved six victories and commanded the *Staffel*. He was a talented musician and an enthusiastic horseman (note the riding crop)

On 8 February 1917 Jakob Wolff crashed his Albatros into some trees, and several photographs recorded the accident. This top view reveals some of the camouflage pattern on the top wing and tail of OAW-built D II 933/16. The tactical band marking on the fuselage was augmented by the number '2' on the forward fuselage

A close-up of Wolff's crashed OAW-built D II 933/16 shows the number '2' on the fuselage and provides details of the interior structure. Wolff emerged unhurt from the accident

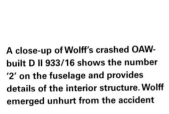

On that same date (8 February) his NCO comrade Vzfw Rieger was also listed with a *zLgzw* claim at Pont-à-Mousson. In an era when the identification of enemy aeroplanes by airmen of both sides was pretty abysmal, Rieger's opponent was merely recorded as a *'Rumpf DD' – Doppeldecker*, or 'solid fuselage biplane'. This indicated that the enemy machine was a conventional aeroplane with an enclosed fuselage and not a *'Gitterschwanz'*.

Finally, on 9 February, Wolff's determination paid off and he was given his first *official* recognition for a victory. Once again he had attacked a Voisin two-seater, shooting it down between Lironville and

The light blue undersides of the wings and tailplane are shown to good advantage in this view of Wolff's crashed D II 933/16. Note that on OAW-built machines the crosses on the underside of the wings still had a white outline, unlike Johannisthal products

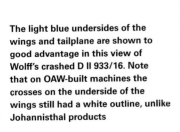

Martincourt, southeast of Pont-à-Mousson. This time there was no dispute about the accuracy of Wolff's claim, and his name duly appeared in the *Nachrichtenblatt* Nr 3. It was the fourth victory credited to *Jasta* 17, but the same day saw a tragic first for the *Staffel* as well. Vzfw Adolph Wellhausen became the first combat casualty of the unit when he was wounded in action near Metz. He died two days later.

Also on 11 February Julius Buckler put in a claim for an enemy aircraft, but as it too fell in French lines he was denied. On the 12th, however, the highly decorated pilot from Baden, Ltn d R Gros, added his name to the *Staffel* lists by downing a Nieuport at Landremont for his first confirmed victory. This was the fifth *Luftsieg* for *Jasta* 17 after three months in combat – a creditable performance by the unit against the French on this stationary front.

The pace of activity was intensifying, with Strasser's logbook revealing 22 flights in February. Between 29 January and 10 February, he had been forced to alternate between D II 1700/16, OAW-built D II 935/16 and his regular mount, D II 1712/16. 16 February saw Strasser make his last flight in his cherished D II 1712/16, and thereafter flew both 1725/16 and 1727/16.

At some point Wilhelm Gros' Albatros D II 1727/16 was repainted with a number '2' instead of a '1', and the crosses were repainted to provide the regulation five-centimetre-wide white border specified by *Idflieg* on 29 October 1916. D II 512/16 is seen on the left, with a white zigzag on a dark band. Georg Strasser flew D II 1727/16 several times in March 1917 (*R Zankl*)

The dark zigzag on a white band was another tactical marking seen on a number of *Jasta* 17 Albatros D II fighters. The D II in the foreground, 1722/16 '2', was flown at least once by George Strasser on a front flight on 28 March 1917. In the background is 518/16 '1', which was possibly flown by both Vzfws Fritz Jacobsen and Rieger at times (*R Zankl*)

An evocative photo of *Jasta* 17 Albatros D IIs on Metz-Frescaty airfield, dwarfed by the massive Zeppelin hangar. In early March 1917 the unit's pilots bid farewell to the well-appointed field at Metz and set out for St Quentin-le-Petit aerodrome on the 7. *Armee* Front

Buckler showed his first victory was no fluke in mid-February. On the 14th he claimed to have brought down a Caudron near Facq Wood, and this time his claim was upheld for his second confirmed kill. The following day he downed yet another Caudron near Pont-à-Mousson, and this was again listed in the *Nachrichtenblatt* as an undisputed victory for Uffz Buckler – his third.

Elsewhere on 15 February, Strasser was flying his usual D II 1712/16 when he engaged two Morane-Saulnier aircraft near Château Salins, but his request for a victory was not upheld. On the 16th Strasser collaborated on a joint *Jagdflug* with Buckler – they fought with three Caudrons and two Moranes without result. Buckler and Strasser were cut from the same cloth, and they were by this time close friends and flying companions. Wasenmüller's accounts recorded 132 flights by *Staffel* pilots in February (contrasted with 81 the preceding month) and a total of 121.5 flying hours. Fifteen aerial combats occurred, and the *Jasta* chalked up four victories.

The first day of March 1917 ushered in a change of great impact for *Jasta* 17. After almost four months of flying in defence of Metz, the *Staffel* was abandoning the expansive field at Metz-Frescaty and making its first move. The unit was ordered to transfer to St Quentin-le-Petit, in the Champagne-Ardennes region on the German 7. *Armee* Front. This transfer was made in anticipation of the coming battle that would be known as the 2nd Battle of the Aisne. A new era was beginning in the history of the *Jasta*, and from this time on it would lead the somewhat nomadic existence expected of many *Jagdstaffeln*.

AIR ACTION ON THE AISNE

S t Quentin-le-Petit is not near the better known city of St Quentin, being further to the southeast close to the River Aisne. It is near the town of Rethel and roughly 60 kilometres northeast of Soissons. Once the pilots and staff of *Jasta* 17 arrived at their new home in early March 1917, they took a few days to get established and to familiarise themselves with the surrounding territory, before commencing operations.

Most of *Rittm* von Brederlow's pilots were also becoming accustomed to new aircraft. The first examples of the latest design from the Albatros stable, the D III, had been acquired even before the *Staffel* left Metz. Georg Strasser recorded his first test flight in the new type on 19 February when he took D III 2032/16 aloft. This machine would subsequently become his usual mount in the months to come. In addition, a photograph exists of Buckler in a newly arrived D III on Metz-Frescaty airfield. This may have been 2033/16, an Albatros that Buckler would make his own and decorate with his usual *Mops* legend. Data in Strasser's *Flugbuch* shows that 2033/16 was on strength by 6 March, and probably earlier.

In addition, a few examples of the LFG Roland D II were on hand. The type's poor performance did not live up to its nickname of *Haifisch* (shark), and it would seem the *Jasta* 17 pilots made limited use of the Roland – no doubt preferring the Albatros machines.

The Albatros D III was in most aspects identical to the D II, except for its sesquiplane (one-and-a-half wing) configuration. Heavily influenced by the success of the French Nieuport fighters, the Albatros designers had

The first of the new Albatros D III fighters were supplied to *Jasta* 17 in February 1917, shortly before the unit left the Metz sector. This D III 2133/16 was damaged in a poor landing by an unknown pilot on Metz-Frescaty aerodrome

In March and April of 1917 *Jasta* 17 was equipped with a mix of Albatros D II, D III and Roland D II types. Here, a *Jasta* 17 Albatros D III has collided with a Roland D II *'Haifisch'*, destroying both machines in the process

This rare photograph shows Julius Buckler warming up the engine of one of the first Albatros D IIIs to arrive at *Jasta* 17. The serial number is not completely visible, but it is possible that this is 2033/16, which Buckler would later mark with his usual *Mops* legend. Note the wooden trestle-type tail support in the right foreground. There was one of these for every aircraft in *Jasta* 17, marked with its serial number. This one belonged to Albatros D II 1705/16

fitted the basic D II fuselage with new single-spar lower wings and 'vee' shaped interplane struts – this improved the pilot's downward visibility from the cockpit. Initially, the D III's flight characteristics and performance surpassed all expectations. However, under the stress of combat manoeuvres, the fatal flaw of the *'Nieuporttyp'* wing cellule would be revealed, as disastrous wing failures began to dog the D III. Nevertheless, after some modifications the type continued to serve, generally achieving a formidable reputation in the spring of 1917.

Jasta 17's activity slackened off a little in March, with 97 hours recorded in just 75 flights, resulting in 11 combats. On 11 March Vzfw Rieger claimed to have destroyed a Nieuport near Cormicy, and this was confirmed in *Nachrichtenblatt* Nr 7 (although some modern sources mark it as unconfirmed). Buckler had a lack of success on the 21st when he attacked a Nieuport without confirmation. Coincidentally, 21 March 1917 was the 48th birthday of the remarkable Jakob Wolff, who was still flying with the *Jasta*. In spite of his advanced age and Jewish ancestry, it seems that Wolff was a respected and popular *Staffel* member – one reason being he kept his comrades well stocked with free cigars from his Hamburg factory!

On 25 March Ltn d R Neumann (a *Kampfstaffel* Metz veteran like Wolff) received credit for a Nieuport fighter as his first victory. That same day Günther Schuster fought a *'Rumpf DD'* at Pontavert, but witnesses for what would have been his second victory failed to materialise and his claim was not upheld.

BLOODY APRIL

April of 1917 has gained a reputation as the nadir in the fortunes of the Royal Flying Corps (RFC) due to the great losses it suffered that month. As the British attempted to dominate the air during the Battle of Arras, the well-equipped German *Jagdflieger* stationed opposite their counterparts in RFC and Royal Naval Air Service (RNAS) squadrons garnered successes and decorations at an unheard of rate.

While *Jasta* 17 was not a participant in the Arras fighting, and remained positioned opposite the French, the unit still had an auspicious month. In fact, the Arras battle was primarily a diversionary assault intended to draw German troops away from the Aisne sector 80 kilometres to the south, where a massive French offensive under Gen Nivelle was planned for mid-April. *Jasta* 17 would be in the thick of that momentous battle.

By this time the *Staffel* was probably primarily equipped with the Albatros D III, along with some remaining D IIs. Strasser's *Flugbuch* indicates that he made almost 40 flights in his favoured D III 2032/16 during April, and only two flights in a D II. However, it was on the second of those two flights in D II 1727/16 (both carried out on 6 April) that Strasser tallied his unit's first kill for the month. On that Good Friday many French fighter pilots were aloft, attacking German captive balloons in an effort to blind the enemy in preparation for the approaching offensive. The German *Jasta* airmen responded to this effort, and a frenetic day of combat ensued.

Strasser was on a patrol with his close friend Buckler, first flying above the clouds and then beneath them, near Berry-au-Bac. As they approached Pontavert, the Württemberger spotted several Caudrons. He made a frontal attack from the left. 'I aim at a distance of ten metres and fire 150 rounds. The Caudron dived and crashed. This is my second aerial victory'.

On Easter Sunday (8 April) Strasser made three flights, the third of which – in D III 2032/16 – lasted 130 minutes. In the margin of his flight log he scribbled, 'My longest duration flight [in a D III]'. He attacked a balloon and a Nieuport during that lengthy mission but failed to destroy either. On the 12th it was Buckler's turn to again lose out on a potential victory when he attacked a Caudron G 4 near Craonne – he put in a claim, but failed to obtain confirmation. On 13 April the Baden native Wilhelm Emmanuel Gros also fought against a Caudron for an unconfirmed claim. That same day Strasser scrapped with a Voisin and two Nieuports, but was unable to bring down any of them.

This line-up of four Albatros D IIs and one D III (third from left) demonstrates the mixed bag of aircraft operated by *Jasta* 17 in April 1917. The photograph may have been taken at Metz, but it is now believed to more likely to show the aerodrome at St Quentin-le-Petit. Most of the machines display the banded markings characteristic of the *Staffel* in this early period

Ltn d R Wilhelm Gros poses for the photographer in his Albatros D III named *Fips*. Many of the aircraft of *Jasta* 17 would be personally baptised with names painted on the fuselage – a practice that was somewhat rare in other *Jagdstaffeln*. Gros claimed to have downed a French Caudron on 13 April 1917, but this was not confirmed

Four stalwarts of *Jasta* 17 pose with an Albatros D III on St Quentin-le-Petit aerodrome. They are, from left to right, Julius Buckler, Heinz Sachsenberg, Wilhelm Gros and Georg Strasser. Buckler claimed an unconfirmed victory on 21 March 1917 and Strasser tallied *Jasta* 17's first victory of 'Bloody April' on the 6th of that month

On 15 April, however, it was an entirely different story – a victory was achieved that became legendary within the unit, and would give Buckler the title for his memoir. He spun a vivid and memorable tale of the events of this day in his book, but his memory played tricks on him and what resulted is a confusing mess that has continued to frustrate historians. Some of Buckler's details simply do not match up with the known facts. It seems very likely that he confused and mingled the events of two different victories into one in his book.

The substantiated *facts* are these – on 15 April 1917, Buckler shot down SPAD VII No 117, flown by Sgt Achille Louis Papeil of the celebrated *Escadrille* N3 (the original *Cigogne* or 'Stork' squadron of Georges Guynemer and many other aces) for his fourth victory. The SPAD VII came down behind German lines and Strasser and Buckler landed nearby. Papeil, although slightly injured, was entertained and feted at the *Jasta* 17 *Kasino* that afternoon before being taken away to captivity. Then, on 12 May 1917, Buckler tallied his seventh victory by downing Nieuport 23 No 3674 of Adj Albin Jaussaud of *Escadrille* N75. This aircraft was also forced down in German territory near La Malmaison, overturning upon landing. Buckler and other *Jasta* 17 pilots soon arrived upon the scene, and many popular photographs were taken of the Nieuport with the prominent '9' on its fuselage – several with a happy Buckler and other *Staffel* 17 pilots grouped around the machine.

What this author, and many other historians, believe happened is that when Buckler was writing (or dictating) the text for '*Malaula!*' he inadvertently confused these two events. There are no known photographs of the captured SPAD, although there is one of Papeil in the company of Buckler, Gros, Strasser and Traeger. Perhaps Buckler referred to his photo albums to spark his memory when producing his book, and the numerous shots of the overturned Nieuport influenced him to combine the events of his fifth and seventh victories in his own mind, for he claimed that Papeil was flying a *Nieuport* (sic) that overturned upon landing. Also, Buckler consistently referred to Papeil as 'Papaine' (sic) in his story – the subtle nuances of French pronunciation and Papeil's 'broad singing accent' being foreign to Buckler's Hessian ears.

With all those caveats in mind, some of Buckler's version of the capture of Sgt Papeil's SPAD on 15 April is worth repeating here;

'We took off at dawn with four machines. After ten minutes we had been scattered to the winds, and I flew west, the rising sun behind me. Since nothing was going on at the front I soon turned back again. Then two machines came toward me that were flying at almost the same altitude. I cautiously turned away to one side until I recognised Strasser and made up my mind to join the two of them. This decision saved Strasser's life.

'I thought I was dreaming when I got a closer look at the machine flying behind and somewhat lower than Strasser. It was a Nieuport! (sic). The Frenchman must have been stalking him unnoticed and was now waiting for the favourable moment to strike, and there was no time to lose. I charged at the lower flying Nieuport (sic) and opened fire, but without success. A jam forced me to break off from him. It was at this critical moment that Strasser pounced on him from above. The Frenchman went into a dive with Strasser and myself behind him.'

Buckler goes on to relate that Strasser also suffered a gun stoppage, and as the German turned for home his opponent, in an 'incredibly skilled manoeuvre', managed to get behind Strasser's Albatros and 'sit on his neck'. Buckler – despite his useless guns – dived on the French machine, whose pilot was so unnerved by the attack that he hastily landed, 'during which he flipped over'.

'The prisoner was a nice young fellow, a sergeant, and a real Frenchman. His name was Papaine (sic), and I was truly thankful that my bullets had missed their mark. It was my greatest victory, and there is no other that I think of with such pure joy.'

Buckler went on to relate that the French pilot had taken a grazing wound to his cheek and he *also* had had a jammed weapon – all three pilots had been bluffing in the same way.

Georg Strasser's *Flugbuch* entry for 15 April offers a laconic, though more reliable, viewpoint on these events. He wrote that he was flying with Buckler when they encountered a SPAD at 0615 hrs. Buckler forced the French fighter down two kilometres south of Prouvais. 'I landed very close by', wrote Strasser. 'The opponent was injured, but he was present that afternoon in our *Kasino* nevertheless'.

According to Buckler, an important incident then ensued. At some point in his translated discussions with the *Jasta* 17 pilots, it seems the captive had referred to his downed aircraft as *'ma Lola'*. Perhaps, if these actually were Papeil's words, his SPAD had carried a personal name – as did many other aircraft in *Escadrille* N3, such as Guynemer's *'Vieux Charles'*. After Papeil was sent off into captivity, Buckler's companions imitated his speech, and his *'ma Lola'* was garbled and corrupted into the nonsense word *'Malaula!'*.

One of Buckler's most famous triumphs was his victory over Sgt Achille Louis Papeil of *Escadrille* N3 on 15 April 1917. The Frenchman suffered a slight grazing wound to his cheek from Buckler's first burst, but he was still entertained at *Jasta* 17's *Kasino*. The unwilling guest is pictured along with four of his hosts – from left to right, Georg Strasser, Papeil, Wilhelm Gros, Alfred Träger and Julius Buckler

'The word pleased us and we liked it so much that from that night on we used it', Buckler wrote. '"Malaula" meant "Go after the enemy!", "Charge!" It became a signal, a battle cry! The battle cry of our *Staffel*.' In this fashion the word become a motto for Buckler and *Jagdstaffel* 17.

The originator of these words, Sgt Achille Louis Papeil, was a 26-year-old from Raffenville. He had been posted to *Escadrille* N3 in early 1917 and was apparently credited with two victories and another forced to land. Papeil escaped from prison camp in September 1917 and returned to service. By 1918 he was an instructor in St Cyr. Buckler recorded that he ran into Papeil again shortly after the armistice on a tram stop on the way from Mainz to Wiesbaden. 'He was still in the uniform of a French aviator, which was reason enough for me to take a close look at him. I recognised him immediately by the scar on his cheek'. The two had a friendly discussion and dinner, before parting ways again.

In his account of his fight with Papeil, Buckler claimed to have been genuinely pleased that his opponent had been captured alive. He repeatedly wrote about his unease and guilt in regard to the business of killing. 'Every victory was celebrated, and although I may have been outwardly happy, I felt sadness within. I thought of the men who had to lay down their lives and of their relatives whom I did not know'. If these really were his true feelings during the war, or were perhaps more prevalent as he recalled events 20 years later, we do not know. Buckler also stated;

'As soft-hearted as what I write about my sorrow and compassion may sound, as soon as I was in the air, I thought of only one thing – victory. My comrades called me *'Bull'*. "Steer" would have been closer to the truth. When I was riled up, I forgot everything. The red, white and blue cockades had the same effect on me as the red cape. So I led a sort of double life. In spite of all my inner gentleness, I was quite the furious fellow.'

─────── SECOND BATTLE OF THE AISNE ───────

On 16 April the Second Battle of the Aisne erupted on the 7. *Armee* Front, just as German intelligence had predicted. French Commander-in-Chief Gen Robert Nivelle finally launched his ill-fated but massive offensive against the German-occupied Chemin des Dames Ridge. This disastrous and titanic struggle (also known as the Nivelle Offensive, but called the *der Doppelschlacht Aisne-Champagne* by the Germans) resulted in some 187,000 French casualties and 163,000 German losses. The horrific losses led to the famous mutinies in the French Army.

French aerial activity was equally as fierce as the ground action, as French fighter squadrons were ordered to assist the offensive with formations of ten or more aircraft. The April skies over the Aisne became as bloody as those flown by the RFC over Arras to the north.

The opening day of the offensive started off with low clouds and rain that limited visibility, but aircraft from both sides were soon braving the elements. Buckler quickly brought his tally to five with a Nieuport destroyed at 1640 hrs near Berry-au-Bac – it was not the only triumph of that day of intense aerial combat. Flying his D III 2032/16 over the inferno of shellfire below, Strasser found himself directly above the French infantry assault near Berry-au-Bac. His log recorded, 'Heavy artillery fire. Sustained enemy aerial activity. At 1120 hrs I shoot down a Caudron in flames'. This was Strasser's third confirmed victim.

Jasta 17's commander *Rittm* von Brederlow contributed to the day's action by claiming a Caudron near Génicourt at 1030 hrs. However, even an aristocratic *Staffelführer's* claims were subject to the same strict confirmation procedures as any other flier in the German Army air service, and von Brederlow's 'victory' apparently went unconfirmed. Much worse befell the aggressive Vzfw Rieger though, for he crashed at Pontavert after a combat, overturning his Albatros D II and breaking his left arm. He may have tangled with Brig Roger Rigault of *Escadrille* N73 (another component of the elite 'Storks' group), who was credited with an enemy aircraft destroyed at 1025 hrs (French time) north of Cormicy. Rieger would soon return to the *Staffel*, still unfit for combat with his arm in a sling, but the details of any further service are unknown.

On 17 April, taking advantage of a lull in aerial activity, Strasser flew over a French aerodrome near Reims to drop a letter from Sgt Papeil to his comrades. Strasser had probably promised to do so when Papeil was entertained in the *Jasta* 17 *Kasino*. Such chivalric courtesies were quite common between the aerial combatants of this era. In the following days Strasser frequently flew with a *Kette* (literally a chain, i.e. a flight) of three aircraft. He often flew with *Rittmeister* von Brederlow and Gros, or Gros and Ltn d R Wolfgang Günther – the latter pilot had arrived from FAA 205 on 16 March. Strasser left on leave on 24 April and would not return to the unit again until 12 May.

After several unsuccessful attempts at balloon-busting, Buckler was finally able to satisfy his 'balloon fever' on 26 April for his sixth victory. The balloon of the 36*e Compagnie des Aerostiers* burned down at 0920 hrs at Bois de Génicourt. The French observer, Sgt Saudet, lost his life.

That same day 48-year-old Vzfw Jakob Wolff again experienced disappointment when he riddled a Caudron G 4, but it came down in

On 16 April *Jasta* 17 commander *Rittm* Heinz Anton von Brederlow attacked a Caudron, but his claim apparently went unconfirmed. The *Staffelführer* is seen here perched on the cockpit rim of his Albatros D III. This machine was marked with black and white bands, roughly in the proportions of the Iron Cross ribbon. This marking would later be seen on other machines of the unit as well

Vzfw Rieger was shot down on 16 April 1917, crashing this Albatros D II. He broke his left arm in the crash

Nursing his broken arm sustained in his crash of 16 April, Vzfw Rieger poses by Julius Buckler's Albatros D III 2033/16 *Mops*

Julius Buckler scored two confirmed and three unconfirmed victories during 'Bloody April'. Seen here is Buckler's famous *Mops*, Albatros D III 2033/16, which he probably flew for most of those combats. This machine still displays the banded identification system instituted at Metz, as well as standard three-colour camouflage on the wings and tailplane. Note the small cockade painted on a patched bullet hole on the vertical stabiliser directly above the 'D' in the fighter's serial. All of Buckler's aircraft were christened *Mops*, although he later had a reserve aircraft named *Lilly*

French lines and it was not credited. Nevertheless, his resilient character came through, and two days later he forced down another twin-engined Caudron at 0830 hrs on a morning patrol. The French craft reportedly fell near to Fort Brimont, allowing Wolff to tally his second confirmed victory. Such success and drive could not be denied, and on 6 May he was promoted to leutnant der landwehr – a rare event for a Jew in the German Army of the day.

As 'Bloody April' ebbed on into May, the men of *Jagdstaffel* 17 encountered both success and adversity as the Nivelle Offensive came to its end. A talented transfer from *Jasta* 1 was posted to the *Staffel* sometime in April. Ltn d R Herbert Schröder had already put his name in the record books during his service with *Jasta* 1 when he destroyed a Sopwith Pup on 4 March for his first confirmed victory. In *Jasta* 17, Schröder would attain no more triumphs before he was sent to a hospital on 1 June, possibly due to illness. He would eventually return to *Jasta* 1 and record the balance of his five victories from July to October 1917.

On the last day of April Julius Buckler put in a claim for a Nieuport, but this was not credited. Buckler wrote that 'our sector of the front fell more and more quietly asleep. May of 1917 was for us the most calm and peaceful May of the war'. On the 6th Buckler had shot up a SPAD VII at Pontavert, but he was credited with only a *zLgzw* aircraft, which was not counted in his official score.

8 May saw Nivelle's costly offensive stall (it was terminated 12 days later). On the 9th *Rittmeister* von Brederlow was wounded in combat, just seriously enough to remove him from command and have him sent to hospital. *Jasta* 17 had lost its well-respected first *Staffelführer*, who was later appointed to a post with *Idflieg*.

There were relatively few qualified candidates for the position of *Jasta* leader within the unit, so the high command brought in someone from outside. Hptm d R Eberhard von Seel was transferred from the prestigious *Jasta* 'Boelcke' to take over *Jasta* 17 on 14 May 1917. Born in Wallmerod on 24 January 1885, von Seel was a veteran of *Infanterie-Regiment* Nr 176. Although he had been with *Jasta* Boelcke only briefly, and as yet had no victories, he did display a certain sense of style, decorating his brand-new Albatros D V (no doubt one of the first in the unit) with highly conspicuous stripes, most likely in the Prussian colours of black and white.

As noted previously, just before von Seel arrived, the ever-aggressive Julius Buckler brought his total to seven confirmed victories when he

This group photograph of *Jasta* 17 personnel was probably taken sometime soon after 6 May 1917 – the date of Jakob Wolff's promotion to leutnant. Standing, from left to right, are Ltn d L Jakob Wolff, Ltn d R Wilhelm Gros, *Rittm* d R Hans *Freiherr* von Brederlow (brother of the CO, who served as adjutant, or *OzbV*, for a time), *Staffelführer Rittm* Anton Heinz *Freiherr* von Brederlow, Ltn d R Heinz Sachsenberg and Ltn d R Herbert Schröder. Seated, left to right, are Vzfw Julius Buckler, Ltn d R Erich Zschunke, Oblt Gunther Viehweger and Ltn Alfred Träger. Note the presence of cigars, liberally furnished by Wolff!

shot down Nieuport 23 No 3674 of Adj Albin Jaussaud of *Escadrille* N75 on 12 May. Jaussaud's Nieuport came down near La Malmaison, and he was taken prisoner. A large crowd soon gathered around the spectacle of the overturned aeroplane and a photographer had a busy time shooting a proud Buckler and his prize. As an aviator, Adj Jaussaud was a relative novice. Born on 24 January 1888, he had gone to war with the *7e regiment du genie*, earning the *Croix de Guerre* with one *palme* and one *étoile de vermeil et 1 étoile d'argent*. He transferred to aviation in September 1916 and had been posted to *Escadrille* N75 on 26 April 1917, falling to Buckler just 16 days later. He died in 1968.

There is a distinct gap in Buckler's victory tally between his seventh claim on 12 May and his eighth which came in mid-July. His sometimes confusing chronology of events related in *'Malaula!'* offers one possible explanation. According to the book, in about mid-May Buckler was ordered to attend a four-week refresher course in fighter pilot training at *Jastaschule* 1. 'With seven victories I held first place in *Jasta* 17, so why of all people was I being sent to a school for fighter pilots?' However, orders were orders. In his confusing account, Buckler stated that on his long flight to the fighter school, he was jumped by three French aircraft and shot

down, with wounds to his lip and left eye. However, for various reasons this cannot be true, and he must have again transposed events – those wounds actually came on 17 July. At any rate, he did complete the course at the *Jagdfliegerschule* and came away with grateful appreciation of the 'higher techniques, so to speak' and 'a lot of theoretical knowledge' that would prove useful later on.

Georg Strasser had returned from his leave on 12 May 1917, only to hear the depressing news that in his absence Ltn d R Wolfgang Günther had wrecked the Württemberger's favourite Albatros D III

Hptm d R Eberhard von Seel was posted to the command of *Jasta* 17 from *Jasta* Boelcke on 14 May 1917. He was soon flying a splendidly decorated Albatros D V, as seen here. It is believed that a unit marking of a black tail had been adopted by this time, and it seems probable that the stripes on von Seel's D V were black and white. This flamboyant décor failed to bring von Seel much luck for he did not attain a single victory, and his tenure as *Staffel* leader would be brief

2032/16. On the 14th Strasser switched to D III 2289/16 and flew that machine primarily for the following days. He made two eventful flights on 23 May, the first of these seeing him test D III 2289/16 in mock combat against a captured Nieuport. Later that day he was flying with Ltn d R Wilhelm Gros when he was roughly handled by two SPADs, Strasser's D III sustaining 15 hits and its rudder being left disabled. The fighter was force-landed south of Hudlicourt, after which D III 2289/16 was shipped off to a *Flugpark* for repairs.

Less than two weeks after von Brederlow was wounded, the *Staffel* suffered another loss when Wolfgang Günther was injured in a crash of an Albatros D III on 21 May. He soon left for the hospital and apparently made a quick recovery, but was posted to *Jasta* 3 on 28 May.

On 30 May two French balloons were destroyed by *Staffel* pilots in a coordinated afternoon attack. The aviators who achieved this success could hardly have been more different – one was a young neophyte and the other was old enough to have been his father. Ltn Albrecht Crüsemann burned a 'gasbag' south of Berry-au-Bac, the 20-year-old pilot having been posted in from AFP 1 on the 7th of the month. A member of *Infanterie-Regiment* Nr 48, he had been born in Heimsen on 17 July 1896 – the balloon was his first, and only, victory. The other balloon credited to *Jasta* 17 that day fell to Ltn d L Jakob Wolff, who was more than twice the age of his comrade Crüsemann. The balloon went up in flames at Boutancourt for Wolff's third confirmed victory.

In exchange for two casualties in May – including the *Staffelführer* – *Jasta* 17 could only mark down one aircraft and two balloons destroyed. Strasser's flight log offers one partial explanation for the waning potency of the unit – he considered the

French SPAD VII superior to the Albatros. In spite of a number of tussles with the enemy, Strasser had not scored since mid-April. He was still flying the Albatros D III, and continued to do so into June – one of his D IIIs was named *Taps*. On 4 June Strasser had a fight with two SPADs, and on the next day he scrapped with what he called a *'Gross-Caudron'* (Large Caudron).

Perhaps another factor in *Jasta* 17's waning fortunes at this time was the diverse variety of fighter aircraft they were expected to fight with. In late May and into early June, Strasser's flight log recorded a trial flight in one of the new D V Albatros types, several missions in Albatros D IIIs' 2177/16 and 2291/16 and even a flight in an old Roland D II *'Haifisch'*. Such a diversity of machines must have been a headache for the unit's mechanics and fitters, at the very least.

Even more troubling was the loss of their second commander. Hptm d R Eberhard von Seel fell less than a month after his arrival, his Albatros D V being shot down in flames during combat with a SPAD at Montigny on 12 June 1917. The *Staffelführer* had had the bad luck to encounter one of the rising stars of *Groupe de Combat* 12, the famous elite 'Storks' fighter wing – von Seel's opponent was none other than Adj-Chef René Fonck. The Frenchman, of course, would go on to survive the war as the Allied 'ace of aces', with 75 confirmed victories, but at this time he was still a newly minted ace with his score standing at five.

After the war Fonck wrote his memoirs, *Mes Combats* (later translated into English as *Ace of Aces*). He was a formidable ace, but in its own way his book is occasionally almost as exaggerated and factually dubious as Buckler's. Still, by examining the date, location and circumstances of the encounter it is certain that Fonck shot down von Seel. The *'Cigognes'* ace related the story of his sixth victory in his usual style;

'I was out on patrol very early on the morning of 12 June and discovered two Albatrosses, which were climbing. Instantly I followed them in their manoeuvres and suddenly pounced on them with the sun at my back. This time I had to deal with two fighter aeroplanes. The latter do not ordinarily withdraw without being forced to do so for pressing reasons. My position was certainly very favourable. I saw them clearly stand out against the sky, which seemed to get lighter at each moment, while they must have had an unclear vision of me in the blinding rays of the sun.

'I realised immediately that I had to deal with two seasoned veterans, but the first appeared to fly straight in the direction of his lines. The other came around to meet me with determination. At the moment I thought I had him, I saw him turn around in a rapid bank. In this way, with one behind me and the other in front, they were going to fire at me together at their ease. I had the impression at that moment that my life was hanging by a thread, and to avoid an immediate bullet, I risked an abrupt turn, which would bring my adversary into my field of fire.

'His next attempt was unfortunate and his bank too slow. I was able to empty my band of cartridges into him broadside. His disabled aeroplane rapidly nose-dived, the pilot himself killed by a bullet in the throat. His companion tried to take advantage of the situation in order to escape me, but it was too late. I immediately overtook him and shot him down, too. He fell in our lines opposite Fort Brimont.

This striking portrait of Ltn d L Jakob Wolff in full flying gear may seem a bit menacing, but it also indicates his resilient and determined character. On 30 May 1917 Wolff achieved his third confirmed victory when he was credited with a balloon destroyed

Jasta **17 lost its second commander on 12 June 1917 when Hptm *d R* von Seel was shot down in his Albatros D V. The *Staffelführer* was the victim of Adj-Chef Réne Fonck of *Escadrille* SPA103, von Seel being the sixth of the French 'ace of aces" 75 confirmed victories. Note the headrest of von Seel's machine, characteristic of early production D Vs**

On 15 June Günther Schuster achieved his second of an eventual six victories when he claimed a 'Caudron' over Berry-au-Bac. Schuster is seen here in the cockpit of his white Albatros D III named *Virginal*. Schuster was an accomplished musician, and the name actually referred to an antique type of small harpsichord dating to the 16th century. Georg Strasser's flight log reveals that he also flew *Virginal* a few times

'Information found on one of my two victims showed that my victory was going to take on the proportions of a catastrophe in Germany. I had brought down Capt von Baer (sic), commanding officer of one of their best fighter squadrons. He had 12 victories to his credit (sic) and was considered one of the enemy's most skillful pilots. I was warmly congratulated.'

Although this account makes for exciting reading, there are some obvious problems with Fonck's narrative. There was no such 'Capt von Baer' in existence. While Fonck claimed *two* Albatros fighters destroyed, the French authorities saw fit to recognise only *one* of them – downed at Cauroy-Cormicy at 0820 hrs. It seems possible that French aerial intelligence had somehow discovered that *Jasta* 17 (a unit that had indeed been operating against French fliers in the area for some time with modest success, and was perhaps not unknown to them) had lost its commander on the day of Fonck's claims, in circumstances that agreed with his description. Fonck and others probably thought that such an accomplished unit *must* have had a famous and formidable leader. Perhaps the flamboyant décor of von Seel's Albatros D V was noted by Fonck and heightened the impression of a great 'ace'. There is no telling where the name 'von Baer' came from, but it made a thrilling story at any rate.

During these trying times in the early summer of 1917, one of the few bright spots in the *Jasta* 17 record book occurred on 15 June when Ltn d R Günther Schuster attacked what he called a 'Caudron' near Berry-au-Bac and shot it down for his second opponent confirmed as destroyed. This may actually have been a Farman F 40 from *Escadrille* F215 of the French 5th *Armée*. The F 40 was a pusher aircraft of *'Gitterschwanz'* configuration, being somewhat similar in appearance to the Caudron G 3 and G 4. The crew of MdL Alexandre Miot (pilot) and Sous Lt Georges Labellie (observer) both perished in the combat.

Two days later, the ranks of *Jasta* 17 were bolstered by two new arrivals. Vzfw Gustav Schniedewind was transferred in from *Jastaschule* 1 and Ltn Wilhelm Becker joined from *Armee-Flug-Park* 1. Neither had any experience as *Jagdflieger,* but Schniedewind in particular was destined to make his mark.

Born on 28 August 1890, Schniedewind initiated his military service at the age of 21 with *Infanterie-Regiment* Nr 97 on 13 October 1911. In August 1914 he entered the war with the *Pionier-Regiment* Nr 25,

Virginal

being promoted to unteroffizier on 7 January 1915. On 1 August 1916, he joined the *Fliegertruppe* and acquired some of his piloting skills at the Grossenhain *Fliegerschule,* as had Buckler. Like most other German airmen, Schniedewind's first service was in a two-seater unit, FA 29, which he joined on 3 May 1917. He must have shown some aggressive promise, for Schniedewind was posted to *Jastaschule* 1 after only a month as a reconnaissance pilot – on 4 June 1917. After a short indoctrination there, he was chosen for *Jasta* 17 and arrived on 17 June.

The third commander of *Jasta* 17 was Ltn d R Ernst Wendler, and like von Seel he came from *Jasta* Boelcke. Ernst Wendler would score no victories, but here he appears every inch the *Jagdflieger* in his highly decorated Albatros D V. As it was flown by the *Staffelführer,* Wendler's D V is referred to as the *'Familienvater'* machine in *Jasta* 17 albums (i.e., the *paterfamilias,* or head of the family). However, it is not known if that name was actually painted on the aeroplane. Note the décor on the uppersurface of the top wing and the two rear-view mirrors

Jagdstaffel 17 was still in need of a *Staffelführer.* The new commander arrived at St Quentin-le-Petit on 19 June, and like von Seel, he had been drawn from the roster of *Jasta* Boelcke. Ltn d R Ernst Wendler was a Württemberger like Strasser. Born in Ulm, Wendler started his training at FEA 3 in August 1915. On 26 January 1916 he was posted to *Kampfstaffel* 14 of *Kampfgeschwader* 3, receiving his Pilot's Badge after two months. By 29 June his service had earned him Württemberg's Gold Military Merit Medal. On the first day of the Battle of the Somme (1 July 1916), Wendler was seriously wounded when his Roland C II was shot down by British DH 2 ace Maj L W B Rees in the action that earned the latter his Victoria Cross.

After his hospitalisation Wendler had a lengthy recuperation in a series of FEA and AFP postings. In November he was awarded the Knight's Cross of the Military Merit Order. Finally, he was ordered to fighter pilot training at *Jastaschule* I on 25 May 1917. After a short time there Wendler joined *Jasta* Boelcke on 7 June, but a mere 12 days later he was ordered to take over *Jasta* 17. His stint there would prove him a capable and respected *Staffel* leader, but one who was never able to collect a confirmed victory himself.

With their new *Staffelführer* firmly in place and with some promising reinforcements in their ranks, the airmen of *Jasta* 17 may have felt themselves ready for any new challenge. It was not long in coming. On 21 June, Strasser's *Flugbuch* records that he took off from St Quentin-le-Petit in his Albatros D III *Mimi* for the last time and flew to Rethel. It is highly likely that he was accompanied by other *Jasta* 17 pilots in their own fighters, including Julius Buckler who had recently returned from the *Jastaschule* training. At Rethel the impedimenta (and perhaps some of the aircraft) associated with a *Jagdstaffel* was soon loaded on railway cars for a trip north. The *Staffel* had received orders to transfer to the German 4. *Armee* in Belgium. According to Buckler's book, the men flew their aircraft north to their new airfield.

Jagdstaffel 17 had been posted to the fiercely contested skies of Flanders. For many ambitious *Jagdflieger,* this was the best place to be – an action-filled front, which suited the daredevils of *Jasta* 17. Their new assignment meant they would be facing the 'sporting' British airmen of the RFC and RNAS, and opportunities for combat, victories and decorations would not be hard to come by. 'Hot days' lay ahead.

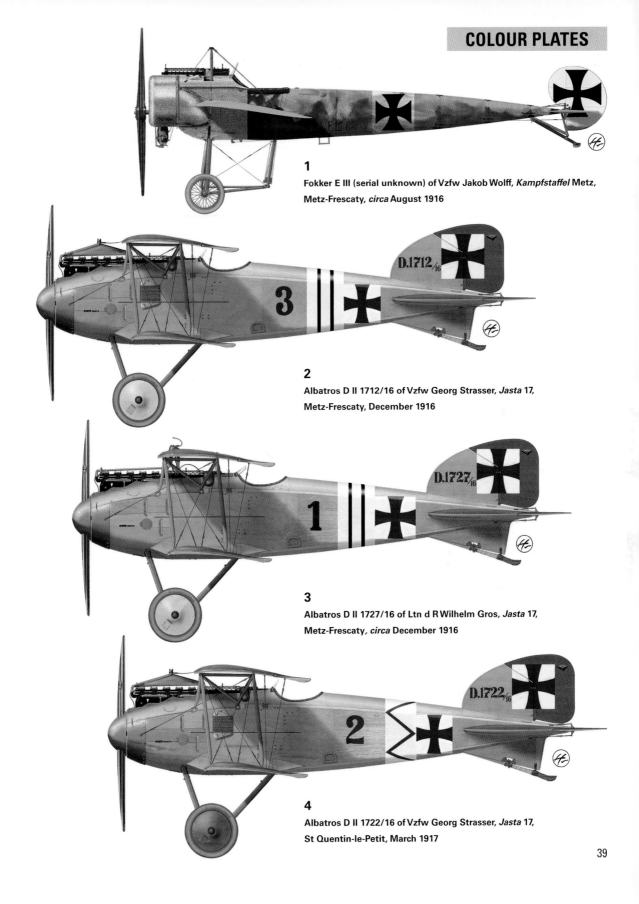

1
Fokker E III (serial unknown) of Vzfw Jakob Wolff, *Kampfstaffel* Metz,
Metz-Frescaty, *circa* August 1916

2
Albatros D II 1712/16 of Vzfw Georg Strasser, *Jasta* 17,
Metz-Frescaty, December 1916

3
Albatros D II 1727/16 of Ltn d R Wilhelm Gros, *Jasta* 17,
Metz-Frescaty, *circa* December 1916

4
Albatros D II 1722/16 of Vzfw Georg Strasser, *Jasta* 17,
St Quentin-le-Petit, March 1917

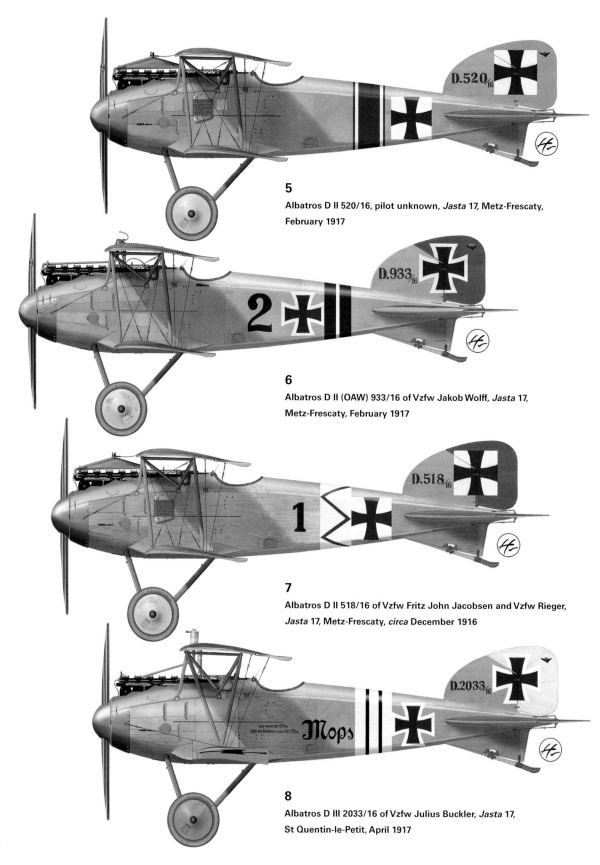

5
Albatros D II 520/16, pilot unknown, *Jasta* 17, Metz-Frescaty,
February 1917

6
Albatros D II (OAW) 933/16 of Vzfw Jakob Wolff, *Jasta* 17,
Metz-Frescaty, February 1917

7
Albatros D II 518/16 of Vzfw Fritz John Jacobsen and Vzfw Rieger,
Jasta 17, Metz-Frescaty, *circa* December 1916

8
Albatros D III 2033/16 of Vzfw Julius Buckler, *Jasta* 17,
St Quentin-le-Petit, April 1917

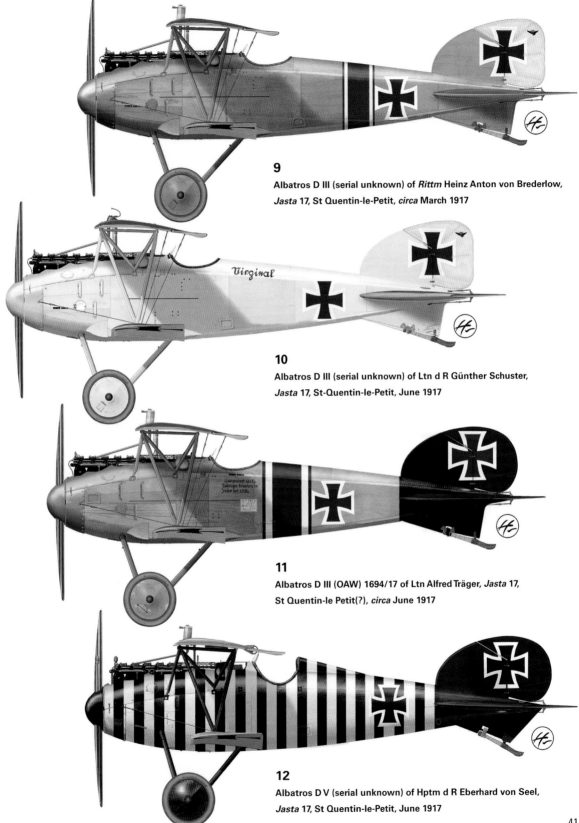

9

Albatros D III (serial unknown) of *Rittm* Heinz Anton von Brederlow, *Jasta* 17, St Quentin-le-Petit, *circa* March 1917

10

Albatros D III (serial unknown) of Ltn d R Günther Schuster, *Jasta* 17, St-Quentin-le-Petit, June 1917

11

Albatros D III (OAW) 1694/17 of Ltn Alfred Träger, *Jasta* 17, St Quentin-le Petit(?), *circa* June 1917

12

Albatros D V (serial unknown) of Hptm d R Eberhard von Seel, *Jasta* 17, St Quentin-le-Petit, June 1917

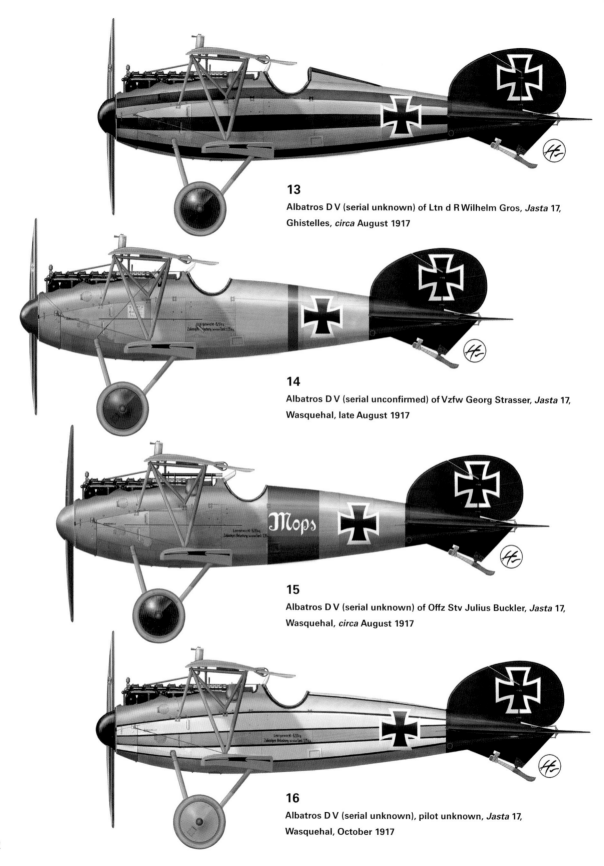

13
Albatros D V (serial unknown) of Ltn d R Wilhelm Gros, *Jasta* 17, Ghistelles, *circa* August 1917

14
Albatros D V (serial unconfirmed) of Vzfw Georg Strasser, *Jasta* 17, Wasquehal, late August 1917

15
Albatros D V (serial unknown) of Offz Stv Julius Buckler, *Jasta* 17, Wasquehal, *circa* August 1917

16
Albatros D V (serial unknown), pilot unknown, *Jasta* 17, Wasquehal, October 1917

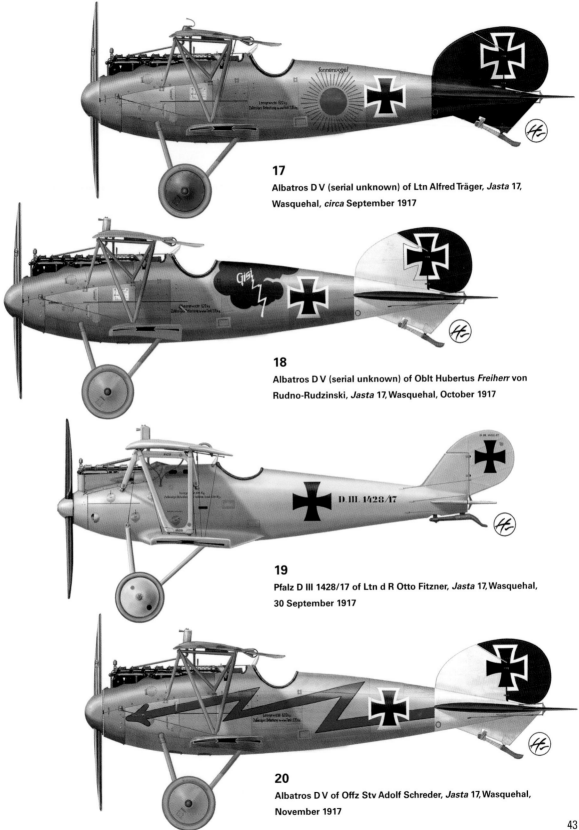

17
Albatros D V (serial unknown) of Ltn Alfred Träger, *Jasta* 17, Wasquehal, *circa* September 1917

18
Albatros D V (serial unknown) of Oblt Hubertus *Freiherr* von Rudno-Rudzinski, *Jasta* 17, Wasquehal, October 1917

19
Pfalz D III 1428/17 of Ltn d R Otto Fitzner, *Jasta* 17, Wasquehal, 30 September 1917

20
Albatros D V of Offz Stv Adolf Schreder, *Jasta* 17, Wasquehal, November 1917

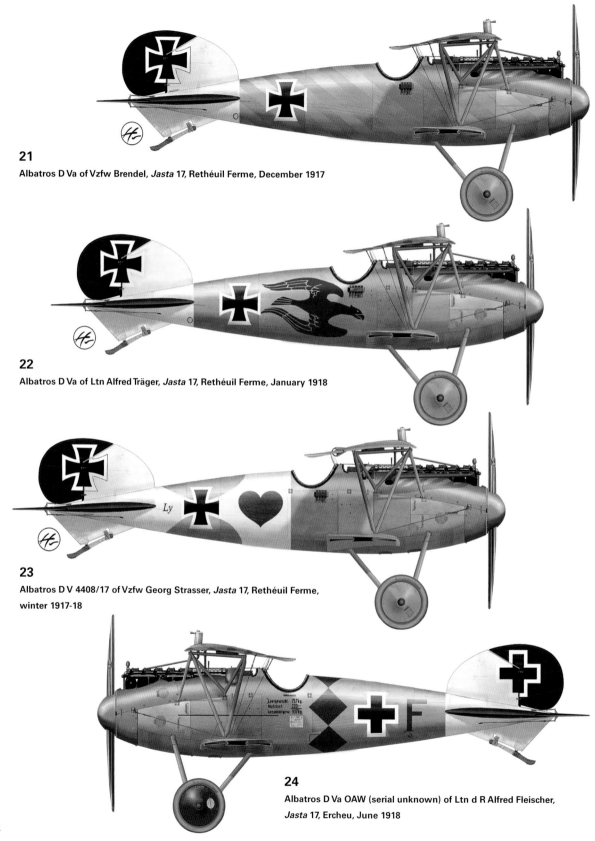

21
Albatros D Va of Vzfw Brendel, *Jasta* 17, Rethéuil Ferme, December 1917

22
Albatros D Va of Ltn Alfred Träger, *Jasta* 17, Rethéuil Ferme, January 1918

23
Albatros D V 4408/17 of Vzfw Georg Strasser, *Jasta* 17, Rethéuil Ferme,
winter 1917-18

24
Albatros D Va OAW (serial unknown) of Ltn d R Alfred Fleischer,
Jasta 17, Ercheu, June 1918

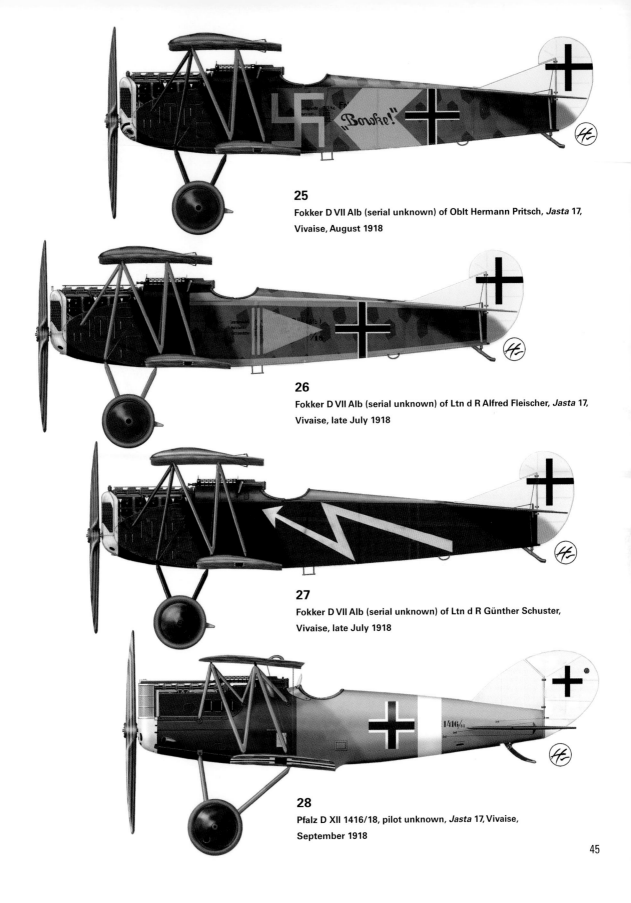

25
Fokker D VII Alb (serial unknown) of Oblt Hermann Pritsch, *Jasta* 17, Vivaise, August 1918

26
Fokker D VII Alb (serial unknown) of Ltn d R Alfred Fleischer, *Jasta* 17, Vivaise, late July 1918

27
Fokker D VII Alb (serial unknown) of Ltn d R Günther Schuster, Vivaise, late July 1918

28
Pfalz D XII 1416/18, pilot unknown, *Jasta* 17, Vivaise, September 1918

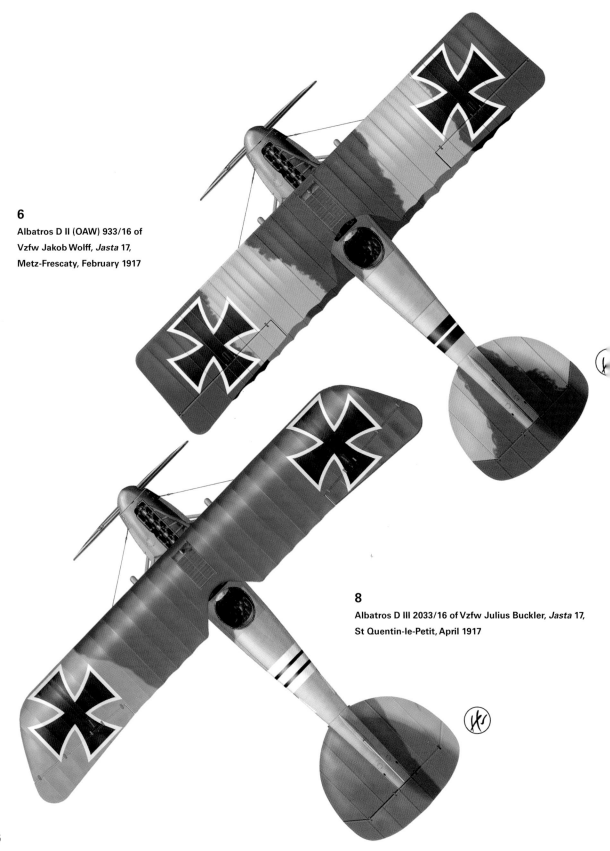

6
Albatros D II (OAW) 933/16 of
Vzfw Jakob Wolff, *Jasta* 17,
Metz-Frescaty, February 1917

8
Albatros D III 2033/16 of Vzfw Julius Buckler, *Jasta* 17,
St Quentin-le-Petit, April 1917

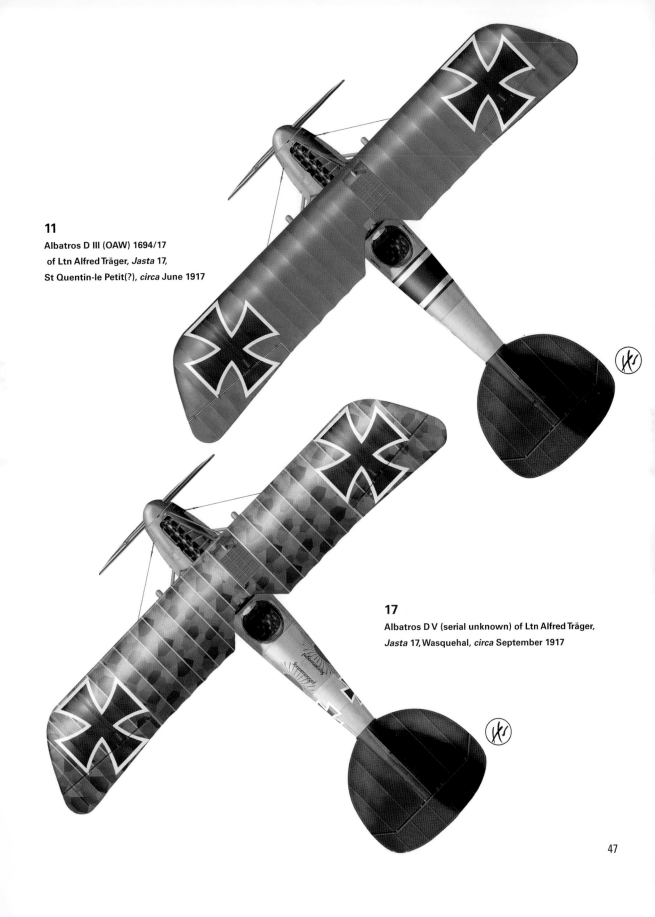

11
Albatros D III (OAW) 1694/17
of Ltn Alfred Träger, *Jasta* 17,
St Quentin-le Petit(?), *circa* June 1917

17
Albatros D V (serial unknown) of Ltn Alfred Träger,
Jasta 17, Wasquehal, *circa* September 1917

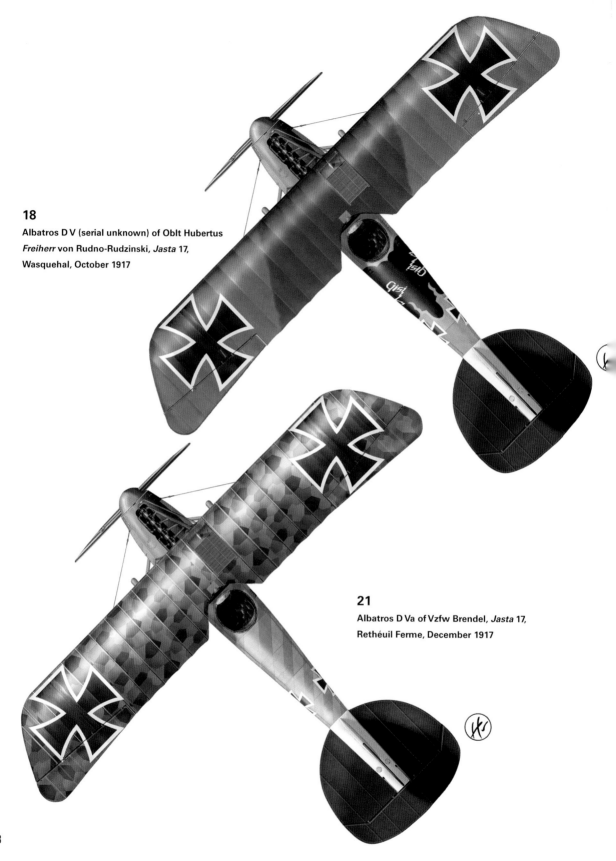

18

Albatros D V (serial unknown) of Oblt Hubertus
Freiherr von Rudno-Rudzinski, *Jasta* 17,
Wasquehal, October 1917

21

Albatros D Va of Vzfw Brendel, *Jasta* 17,
Rethéuil Ferme, December 1917

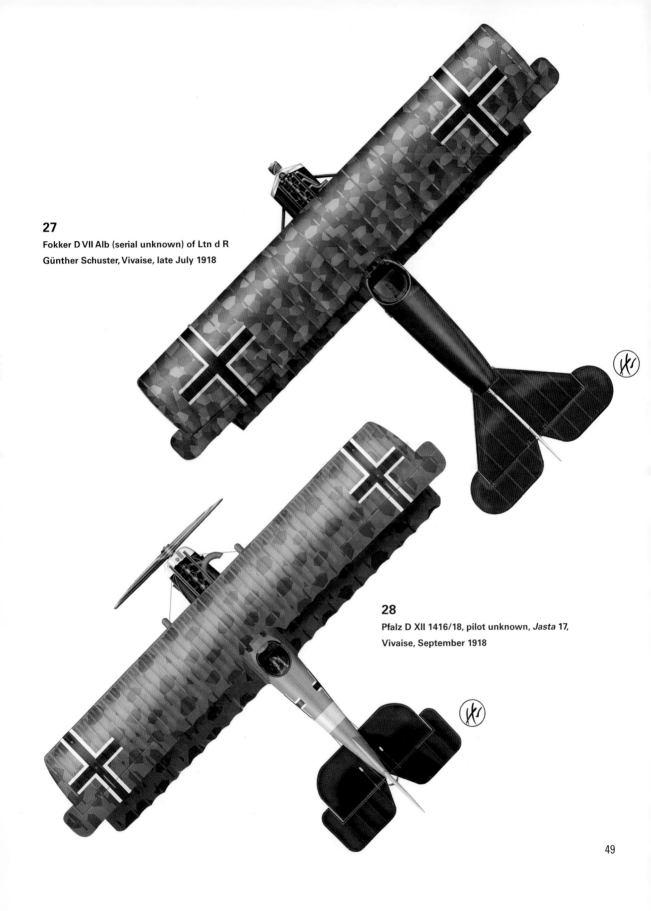

27
Fokker D VII Alb (serial unknown) of Ltn d R
Günther Schuster, Vivaise, late July 1918

28
Pfalz D XII 1416/18, pilot unknown, *Jasta* 17,
Vivaise, September 1918

FIGHTS OVER FLANDERS

The transfer of *Jasta* 17 to Flanders was carried out to supply reinforcements in response to a British offensive in the Ypres sector. The famous Battle of Messines, in which the British detonated 400 tons of ammonal under German positions, commenced on 7 June and ended one week later.

Jasta 17 had completed its move to its new airfield at Ghistelles by 24 June, with Strasser recording his first flight from the new base the next day. Its area of responsibility on this front covered a line from Dixmude to Nieuport to Ostend. By the end of the month this was extended to the line of Ostend-Bruges-Gand. Wendler's pilots would now be opposed by the aggressive squadrons of the RFC and RNAS. Buckler and his comrades would also encounter airmen from the *Aviation Militaire Belge,* as well as a few French *escadrilles* that had been posted to the area. *Jasta* 17 was now part of a temporary grouping known as *Jagdgruppe Nord,* which also included *Jagdstaffeln* Boelcke, 20, 28 and *Kest* 8 under the command of Hptm Otto Hartmann.

Buckler described the new Front;

'The Flanders town to which we moved was called Ghistelles. One could hardly imagine a nicer airfield than the one we found here, with spacious tents and even a [permanent] hangar, while the seaside resort of Ostend lay right next door. Nevertheless, I have only seen the town from above. Already, the increased roar of the artillery fire indicated to us that there would be plenty for us to do in this sector.

'The first orientation flight of the *Staffel* was an experience for me, as I saw the sea for the first time. While the others flew behind the *Staffelführer* out toward the open sea without hesitation, I first had to fight against a very unpleasant feeling inside which wanted to prevent me, a landlubber, from flying over the water. On the return flight we

Jagdstaffel **17 completed its move to Ghistelles by 24 June 1917 and began the process of assembling its aircraft and readying the airfield for action. This panoramic view of the Ghistelles aerodrome shows a number of *Jasta* 17 Albatros D IIIs and D Vs which have yet to have their lower wings affixed. All display the black tail unit of the *Staffel*. (*1914 Aviation Heritage Trust*)**

encountered [German] warships and flew towards them with joyful greetings. From now on whenever we went into our [landing] glide we found ourselves above the sea, which crashed and foamed below us.'

By the beginning of July aerial activity was heating up, with the *Staffel* pilots often flying three times a day. The British were making massive preparations for a series of major offensives in Flanders that would be collectively known as the Third Battle of Ypres (or the Battle of Passchendaele). Ghistelles airfield was very close to the frontlines, and *Jasta* 17's airmen and groundcrews discovered that it was frequently the target of British bombers. On 3 July Ltn Albrecht Crüsemann claimed an aircraft shot down over the British lines, but failed to achieve confirmation. Five days later Ltn d R Otto Fitzner was posted in from AFP 4 in Ghent, the replacement pilot being destined to chalk up three victories in *Jasta* 17 in coming months before eventually commanding *Jasta* 65, where he would attain his final six kills.

On 9 July Strasser acquired new Albatros D V 2025/17. It immediately became his regular machine, Strasser completing more than 30 frontline flights – and scoring two victories – in the fighter over the next seven weeks.

There were rainstorms all day on 10 July, but they did not prevent some tremendously significant fighting that resulted in *Jasta* 17's first victory on this Front. The Allied air offensive in support of the planned ground attack had been scheduled to begin on 8 July, but it had been delayed by bad weather. The Germans struck first with a pre-emptive strike against the British Fourth Army in an unprecedented, and superbly coordinated, action involving army, naval and air forces. Codenamed *Unternehmen Strandfest* (Operation 'Beach Party'), it started with a fierce bombardment that began in the morning and lasted for 13 hours.

Aircraft from FAA 231 and Numbers I and II *Marine Feldflieger Abteilungen* attacked the British lines, directing artillery fire that destroyed all of the bridges on the River Yser. At 1951 hrs troops from the III *Marine-Infanterie* Division attacked, supported by aircraft. The western bank of the Yser was bombed by 24 German two-seaters, and one aeroplane from II MFA flew above it all and coordinated the action with wireless messages. Escorted by fighters from *Jasta* 17, bombers from *Kampfgeschwader* (KG) 1 attacked between the coast and Lombardsijde-Oostduinkerke, dropping some 2750 kg of bombs. Four bombers flew ahead of the attacking naval infantry, strafing the enemy with 3100 rounds – at times from a height of just 20 metres.

Ghistelles aerodrome is the location of this superb shot of *Jasta* 17 fighters, all showing the black tail unit marking. In the foreground is an Albatros D V marked with lengthwise white stripes with narrow black edging (*1914 Aviation Heritage Trust*)

On the evening of that rainy day of intense conflict, Strasser flew his third sortie of the day over the Ypres Canal – a flight that lasted an impressive 130 minutes. In his usual laconic style, he wrote in his *Flugbuch*, 'Escorting bombers from KG 1. *Luftkampf* with Nieuports and Sopwiths. At an altitude of 3500 metres I shoot down a Sopwith using 300 rounds. My fourth aerial victory'.

There are two possibilities regarding what particular Allied machine might have constituted Strasser's victory, recorded as a 'Sopwith 2' (two-seater) downed at 2100 hrs. Some think that his victim was a Morane-Saulnier P rotary-engined two-seater from *Escadrille* N31. MdL Charles Gauthier (pilot) and Soldat Abel Denis (gunner) were reported missing in Morane Parasol No 937, making a forced landing in the German lines at Bersée at 1040 hrs. Both crewmen survived as prisoners, and their intact Morane – still displaying the 'Greek archer' insignia of *Escadrille* 31 – was flown to the *Jastaschule* 1 at Valenciennes.

Some historians, however, equate Strasser's claim with a Sopwith Camel of 4 Naval Squadron that was shot down fighting against four enemy aircraft near Ramscapelle. Flt Sub-Lt E W Busby was killed in Camel N6361 – he was the very first Camel casualty in combat. 4 Naval Squadron, based at Bray Dunes, had been the first unit to be equipped with the nimble Sopwith fighter. On 10 July, a patrol of the new Camels had attacked three twin-engined German bombers over Coxyde when ten Albatros fighters intervened. Busby's Camel was attacked by four of the German scouts over Pervyse, and it was seen to go down minus a wing.

What is certain is that by noon on 11 July German troops had seized positions on the eastern bank of the Yser from the coast to Nieuport, and the British had lost 126 officers and 3000 men in just two days of fighting.

Although Strasser had claimed the first 'Flemish' victory for *Jasta* 17, it was the ever-aggressive Julius Buckler who would down the lion's share

Julius Buckler would chalk up six victories during his unit's stay at Ghistelles, scoring four times in July and twice in early August. He is seen here with his Albatros D V *Mops*

of opponents in the coming weeks. His eighth victory was a Sopwith Triplane of the RNAS, shot down south of Zillebeke. Confusingly, this victory is dated as 12 July in the *Jasta* 17 record book, but as 11 July in the *Nachrichtenblatt*. It was officially recorded as Buckler's eighth confirmed claim.

His next victory was an 'FE' claimed on 13 July at 1320 hrs near Stuivekenskerke for his ninth success. What Buckler probably shot at was a Farman F 40 of the Belgian *2me Escadrille*. The crew of Sous Lt Etienne de Robiano and Lt Roméo Verhagen were attacked by Buckler's Albatros and forced to land inside their own lines at Ferme Grand Cambron, near Oostkerke. Their Farman was destroyed but both crewmen were unhurt. That same 'Friday the 13th' Strasser attacked a Sopwith Pup above the British lines near Bruges. The fighter was brought down, but a competing claim was put in by Ltn d R Gerhard Flecken of *Jasta* 20. The victory was awarded to Flecken by the authorities – his second of four eventual successes.

Buckler's next opponent left him with such vivid memories that he recounted the tale in print at least three different times in the 1930s – each one a bit different from the others. Besides telling the story in *'Malaula!'*, he also gave a version to German historian Walter Zuerl, who wrote a narrative that appeared in his book

Pour le Mérite Flieger (1938). Buckler was also interviewed by, or corresponded with, American writer James Perley Hughes for the aviation 'pulp' magazine *War Birds,* and a highly coloured account of the same fight turns up in an article about Buckler in the August 1934 issue.

The simple facts are that on 14 July at 1750 hrs, Buckler shot down Martinsyde G102 'Elephant' No A6266 flown by 2Lt C M De Rochie of No 27 Sqn RFC, who was killed, near Leffinghe. By selecting the most reliable and confirmable details in the varied accounts, the story of the ace's tenth victory can be told while preserving a bit of the flavour of Buckler's retellings.

14 July was an oppressive, stormy day with a strong northwest wind. Buckler was sitting in his shirtsleeves in the pilot's *Kasino,* gazing out at the lowering sky watching the lightning flash between the thunderclouds. The occasional brief shower seemed to indicate that there would be

This group portrait was taken at Ghistelles, most likely on the steps of the pilots' *Kasino*, at some time between 10 and 17 July 1917. Offz Stv Julius Buckler is seated on the bottom step. The three men seated immediately behind him are bareheaded Vzfw Gustav Schniedewind (left), Ltn d R Günther Schuster and Vzfw Adolf Werner behind them. The remainder, standing, from left to right, are Ltn d R Otto Fitzner, Vzfw Georg Strasser, *Staffelführer* Ernst Wendler, Ltn d L Jakob Wolff, Ltn d R Walter Brachwitz, Ltn Wilhelm Becker, Ltn d R Zschunke and Ltn d R Ehlers. Finally, Ltn Alfred Träger is sitting on the balustrade. Of this group, Buckler was the leading scorer, attaining his eighth and ninth victories between 11 and 13 July. Schniedewind would get his first victory of seven on 21 July, and Fitzner and Strasser would also become aces (*L Bronnenkant*)

no air combat that day. Then suddenly the big sheepdog 'Greif' (a pet of Ltn Alfred Träger's) became restless and perked up his ears. According to Buckler, 'Greif's' sharp ears could always pick up the engine noise of approaching British bombers before any forward listening post did. 'All of my drowsiness disappears in a flash', wrote Buckler. He shouted to the mess orderly, 'Behle, go! Call and tell them to get *Mops* ready!'

Soon the sound of anti-aircraft fire confirmed Buckler's trust in the hound's instincts, as a report came in that a British bomber had been sighted. As the sheepdog bounded toward the air-raid shelter, Buckler raced across the airfield to his Albatros D V, which was awaiting him with engine running. 'I climbed into *Mops* with just shirt, trousers, scarf and goggles on and flew towards Bruges. There was still lightning, and the raindrops stung my face like needles. At 200 metres I plunged into the clouds. I saw a hole, pushed through and then entered the clouds again, climbing even higher. Finally, at 3200 metres, I had blue sky and brilliant sunshine above me'.

In the direction of Bruges, at about 4500 metres, Buckler spotted the black detonations of German flak shells. He soon sighted a British aircraft, apparently about to turn for home. So there he was, 'the enemy I was looking for. He was flying 200 metres higher than I, and as I followed him I pushed my *Mops* to 2000 revs. Then I pulled up and shot at him from below'. Buckler recalled that the enemy pilot was clearly his equal, and that both pilots 'wrung the utmost out of their machines' – he was soon bathed in sweat. They tussled from 4300 metres down to about 3000 metres, with neither gaining an advantage.

'I pretended to make a run for it, and he dived after me. Then I made a sudden turn and he raced past me and, sitting on his neck, I fired a few well-aimed rounds from 15 to 20 metres range. His machine emitted smoke and then burst into flames. Now came the most horrifying thing I have ever experienced in my flying career. I saw the pilot stand up – the brave man did not want to burn – preferring a leap to his death from 3000 metres rather than endure a death by fire. I cannot describe my emotions

Wilhelm Gros was another highly competent airman and *Kette* leader of the *Jasta*. On 17 July 1917 Gros was leading one *Kette* while Buckler led another when they tangled with Sopwith Pups from No 54 Sqn, resulting in Buckler's 11th victory. Here, Ltn d R Gros is pictured with his superbly decorated Albatros D V, which was another example of the early machines with a headrest fitted aft of the cockpit

as I watched this person plunging into the depths before my eyes. I cursed the war. First my fellow aviator and then his burning machine plunged into the seas of cloud, with me following. When I again appeared from out of the clouds I just managed to see the burning motor, with the spark-scattering remains of the airframe whirling around it, strike the earth.

'The spot below me – it was our airfield – was black with people. Then I realised that they were infantrymen who, probably just as paralysed with horror as my *Staffel* mates, first saw a person and then a flaming aircraft plummet from the clouds. None of them could know who the vanquished was.'

Drained, Buckler landed his *Mops* back at Ghistelles. There he sat, 'having remained sitting in my machine after landing, deeply disturbed and pale with horror', until a crowd of his comrades and infantrymen pulled him out and carried him off on their shoulders. A search turned up the charred Beardmore engine of the Martinsyde four kilometres away from the *Staffel* airfield. The body of 2Lt De Rochie was pulled from the nearby Yser Canal – 'not the least disfigured, he looked as if he were sleeping'. Buckler, learning that his fallen opponent had the Gallic sounding name De Rochie, assumed that his victim was a Frenchman.

Curtis Matthew De Rochie, however, was a Canadian from Cornwall, Ontario. He had taken off from his airfield in Martinsyde G102 A6266, having been ordered to bomb Zarren – although the Martinsyde 'Elephant' was a single-seater, it was employed primarily as a bomber. De Rochie had a reputation among his squadronmates as a courageous comrade. Indeed, fellow No 27 Sqn pilot Leslie Campbell recalled that only a week before De Rochie's death, the Canadian had saved his life. Campbell had been cut off alone behind German lines, and two Albatros pilots in their 'painted devils' had been riddling his Martinsyde. Suddenly Campbell saw one of his squadron's machines diving by him with Lewis gun blazing. 'I noted the pilot was bareheaded and knew that it was a Canadian named De Rochie'. The latter had turned back from the safety of Allied lines to rescue Campbell, who never forgot him. A week later De Rochie was buried at Leffinghe by his respectful enemies.

At some point around mid-July 1917 Buckler was promoted to offizier-stellvertreter but the exact date remains unknown. On 17 July he downed another courageous British airman for his 11th victory. Early that Sunday morning, 'We had received orders to fly a "barrage patrol" ['*Sperre*'], which meant seeing to it that no enemy fliers flew over our lines', wrote Buckler. 'During this patrol Ltn Gros led the first *Kette* [flight] and I the second. While flying back and forth we ran across six English Sopwiths in the immediate vicinity of our airfield, and at once a most wonderful aerial battle broke out. We were equal in numbers, and the one I took on began to smoke after a few seconds but – thank God – without catching fire. It landed with a total smash-up on our airfield. The other five got away.

'The English pilot, in the meantime, had been pulled from the wreckage of his aircraft with a nasty wound to his right thigh from a ricochet, and he was taken by car to the military hospital in Ghistelles. Afterwards, the poor fellow's right leg was amputated. He was a charming, strapping fellow.'

Buckler could not recall the name of his victim, but postwar research has identified him as Englishman 2Lt Clifford T Felton of No 54 Sqn, who was brought down in Sopwith Pup B1713. Felton survived the amputation of his leg, and captivity, to give his own statement about the fight upon his repatriation from prison camp in January 1918. He was in one of four Pups on an offensive patrol, 'when enemy machines were sighted. We attacked, and during the fight, when I was behind an enemy machine, I was hit by a piece of high explosive shell that badly shattered my leg. The shock was great, and this made it impossible to continue.

'Just then I was attacked unobserved, and apparently at close range, by an enemy machine, and bullets hit my petrol tank and set the machine on fire. I side-slipped down at a steep angle, trusting it would bring me to our lines and try to extinguish the flames. However, a few seconds before I reached the ground the flames appeared to have died down, with part of the machine only smouldering. I pulled back on the control, and much to my surprise the machine pulled up slowly and turned over on its back.

'After the crash landing I unfastened my belt and dropped into what turned out to be water. I then guessed where I was, and in about a quarter of an hour's time one of the enemy waded in and I was conveyed to a barge along the canal, which runs close by the flood at Nieuport, and taken to a field hospital, when I became unconscious for a time.'

After his leg was amputated, Felton was taken to Munster Hospital, and then to the Prisoner of War (PoW) camp at Karlsruhe.

All available research indicates that Buckler was also wounded on 17 July (most likely in the scrap with the Pups from No 54 Sqn), although he made no mention of it in his description of that day's fight. These wounds were probably the ones he noted much earlier in his book, and described out-of-sequence. 'My upper lip was closed with 14 stitches and the gaping laceration above my left eye with 26'. Buckler's recuperation did not take too long. In fact Strasser's log book records a flight made with him on 28 July. Once again, Buckler's confusing and contradictory accounting in 'Malaula!' leaves historians puzzled and frustrated.

On 21 July Uffz Gustav Schniedewind downed a Sopwith at 1530 hrs at Nordschoote for his first confirmed triumph.

25 July was scheduled to have been the opening day of the Battle of Ypres, but British aerial observation crews discovered that the Germans had pulled back many of their batteries to the safety of the rear areas. The offensive was postponed so that British guns could be moved forward and RFC squadrons sent out to discover the new German artillery positions for counter-battery fire. On the 27th, reconnaissance flights revealed that the Germans had made a significant withdrawal, so the offensive was again postponed until the 31st so that British batteries could be re-located yet again.

During the afternoon of 27 July, DH 4 bombers of No 55 Sqn were carrying out a raid on Gontrode when *Jasta* 17 attacked them south of Dixmude. Vzfw Werner apparently shot down one of them for his second confirmed victory in 11 days.

On 27 July 1917 Jakob Wolff tallied his fourth, and final, victory with *Jasta* 17, but he was himself wounded in the combat and would never return to the front. This portrait was taken after the war when he was near – or past – 50 years of age. The former pacifist displayed considerable pride in his decorations, and the more relaxed post-war atmosphere allowed him to arrange them as he saw fit. He chose to wear his prized Knight 2nd Class with Swords of the House Order of the White Falcon at his neck (as if it were a Commander's badge) and not on the *Grossordensschnalle* on his left breast as wartime regulations specified (*N W O'Connor*)

That same day a *Jasta* 17 pilot who must have been something of a legend within the *Staffel* made his last mark in the unit's tally book. Ltn d L Jakob Wolff was now four months past his 48th birthday, but he was still flying and fighting. One of the very few veterans of *Kampfstaffel Metz* left with the *Jasta,* Wolff had proven all the doubters wrong by bravely performing his duties with the unit since its inception. On 27 July he finished off an enemy aircraft at 1615 hrs, his opponent being listed as a Farman. He had most likely attacked a Farman F 40 of the Belgian *3me Escadrille* – the crew of 1er Sgt Jean Meeus and Lt Robert Mongenast were flying a machine that was severely shot up over Eesen. It was confirmed as Wolff's fourth victory.

Unfortunately, 'Papa' Wolff was himself wounded badly enough by Mongenast's defensive fire to be hospitalised in Ghistelles for lengthy treatment. He would never return to active service. By 1918 Wolff was back running his cigar factory in Hamburg.

Having lost its most veteran pilot on the 27 July, *Jasta* 17 suffered a fatality the following day. Albrecht Crüsemann, who had been with the unit less than 11 weeks and had one victory to his name, was flying over Nieuport with Buckler and Strasser according to the latter's *Flugbuch*. Crüsemann attacked a SPAD, but his combat manoeuvres were so stressful that a wing tore loose from his fighter. The Achilles' heel of the Albatros D III and D V – wing failure – had claimed another *Jagdflieger*. Crüsemann's crippled machine plunged into the sea northwest of the Nieuport Mole.

THIRD BATTLE OF YPRES

On 31 July the long-delayed Third Battle of Ypres (or the Battle of Passchendaele) finally commenced. On the opening day low clouds and mist hampered aerial operations. As the rains poured down for the next five days the British Army was stopped in its tracks and almost no war flying was possible. The rains turned the battleground into a quagmire – August of 1917 was the rainiest August of the preceding 30 years.

According to Wasenmüller, in July *Jagdstaffel* 17 completed 396 flights and logged 394.75 flying hours. No fewer than 98 aerial combats were recorded (by far the highest number of any month thus far in the war) and nine victories were confirmed. In August the number of combats would reach a zenith of 195, and even as the terrible weather conditions hampered flying the *Staffel* logged 399 flying hours.

Up to 9 August rains severely limited flying in the Ypres sector. Although there were still rainstorms of the 9th, a great deal of flying was done and the RFC suffered 14 casualties. The Mainz native nicknamed 'Bull' by his comrades was responsible for one of those losses. Early in the morning Buckler shot a Sopwith down in flames southeast of Nieuport at 0745 hrs, 9 Naval Squadron losing Flt Sub-Lt M G Woodhouse in Camel B3870. Buckler increased his total to 13 two days later. On 11 August, Lts D B Davies (pilot) and R H Sawlor (observer, a Canadian) of No 52 Sqn took off on an artillery observation patrol at 1240 hrs (British time) in RE 8 A4645. Buckler engaged the aeroplane west of Spermalie about one hour later and shot it down east of the lines. Both crewmen paid for their devotion to duty with their lives, but the next day the same fate nearly befell their victor.

Buckler was proving to be a real *Kugelfanger* ('bullet catcher' in soldiers' slang), as he was wounded yet again on 12 August. Unfortunately, details about this particular incident are few and difficult to substantiate. His injuries were severe enough to take him out of action for about five weeks. He may have given some pertinent details in his account in *'Malaula!'*, but once again his story cannot be

One of the *Staffel* automobiles provides an opportunity for the photographer at *Jasta* 17's Ghistelles airfield. Seated in front, from left to right, are Wilhelm Becker, unknown and Günther Schuster. From left to right in the vehicle are Alfred Träger, unknown, Georg Strasser, unknown and Ltn d R Ehlers. On 17 August 1917 Ltn Becker shot down a Sopwith for his first confirmed victory

substantiate. Without supplying the date of the incident, he wrote, 'On his day I was flying alone and encountered two Sopwiths at the front. They thought that with their combined force they would make short work of me, but they were fooling themselves. It did not take me long to gain a height advantage, and therewith the upper hand.

'One of them appeared to turn away, but did not think at all of flying home and instead started to climb. I observed him closely, and likewise climbed. At 4500 metres we had approached to within 150 metres of each other. I wanted to wait a bit more, but at this distance – my opponent was definitely using a telescopic sight when he fired – my machine was hit by a salvo and I felt a horrible blow to the left side of my chest.

'I raced at about 2000 revs down to 100 metres, levelled the machine and began to glide. I was rendered temporarily unconscious during this dive, but like a miracle I came to at the right time. The lining of my coat was turned outwards and blood oozed red out of the hole. I could hardly lift my left arm. This was no time for an emergency landing amidst the shell holes! Without the customary circuit of honour around the airfield, which usually signified a victory, I landed with my last ounce of strength.

'"Stretcher!" I yelled to Roth. The medical orderlies were already rushing over with the stretcher, and they lifted me out and carried me to the truck. I was brought to the military hospital in Bruges.'

Buckler's presence would be sorely missed. The next day (13 August) Georg Strasser succeeded in taking up some of the slack. Flying D V 2025/17, he wrote, 'At 2000 metres I attack a Martinsyde, hitting its engine'. The enemy machine went down at Oostdunkerke at 0925 hrs for his fifth confirmed *Luftsieg*. His victim may actually have been DH 4 A7475 from No 55 Sqn, which was returning from a bombing raid to Deynze when it was attacked by German fighters over Roulers and was seen to nose-dive in flames. The pilot, Capt P G Kirk, was killed, as was his observer Lt G Young-Fullalove, who jumped from the aircraft.

14 August was another day of rotten weather, with high winds, rain and low clouds, but aerial combat went on without letup. 9 Naval Squadron apparently lost another Camel to *Jasta* 17, Ltn d R Otto Fitzner, who had joined the unit on 8 July, downing Camel B3820 west of Slype. The pilot, Flt Sub-Lt M N Baron, was last seen going down in a spin after being shot

In late August the *Staffel* moved to Wasquehal airfield, near Lille. Here, Georg Strasser poses with his groundcrew in front of his D V at Wasquehal. Note the dark fuselage stripe that was a personal emblem. While the serial number is not visible, it is likely that this is D V 4408/17 in its first guise. Either that or it may be 2025/17, which Strasser flew to Wasquehal on 27 August 1917, but which was soon replaced by 4408/17

up by an Albatros near Nieuport. He was killed in action, B3820 being the first of nine eventual victories for Fitzner.

On 16 August – the first day of the phase of the Ypres offensives known as the Battle of Langemarck – *Jasta* 17 suffered another casualty. Ltn d R Ehlers, who had only arrived the previous month, was lightly wounded in action despite the famous 'Flanders fog' hampering aerial activity by both sides. It is thought Ehlers returned to the front sometime in September.

By 17 August the Battle of Langemarck was already coming to its end, yet the battles in the sky continued to increase in their ferocity. That day Ltn d R Wilhelm Becker, who had joined the *Staffel* exactly two months earlier from AFP 1, recorded his first confirmed *Luftsieg* when he downed a Sopwith northeast of Cortemarck at 2125 hrs. This may have been Camel N6334 from 6 Naval Squadron, whose pilot, Flt Sub-Lt Strathy, was killed near Zevecote. Two days later, fellow relative newcomer Ltn Walter Brachwitz chalked up his first victory when he downed Bristol F 2B A7171 from No 48 Sqn on a morning patrol. The crew of 2Lt R Dutton (pilot) and 2Lt H R Hart-Davies were returning from an escort mission over Ostend when they encountered Brachwitz, the 'Brisfit' crashing at Oudenberghe. Dutton was killed and Hart-Davies rendered unconscious by injuries suffered in the crash, and he was duly taken into captivity.

Another newcomer had arrived from the *Jastaschule* on 18 August in the form of Offz-Stv Adolf Schreder. Born on 14 December 1888, he would make himself known with a bright lightning bolt emblazoned on his Albatros fighter, and would attain one confirmed *Luftsieg* in 1918.

22 August was a day of bright sun and clear skies that brought the RFC out in great force, resulting in *Jasta* 17 losing one of its most stalwart and respected veterans. A superb pilot who had been with the *Staffel* from the outset, Wilhelm Emmanuel Gros had served as a *Kette* leader and was a steady, reliable comrade. During a dogfight against the Bristol F 2Bs of No 48 Sqn over Vlissegem at 1105 hrs, the 25-year-old Badener was shot down. His body was recovered and returned to his birthplace of Karlsruhe for burial with full military honours.

Four days later the *Jasta* ranks were further depleted when neophyte fighter pilot Uffz Carl Conradt was killed between Slype and Vlissegem at 2040 hrs. He had almost certainly been shot down by two future French aces of *Escadrille* N48, Adj Gilbert de Guingand and Sgt René Montrion, who shared credit for an Albatros D III destroyed north of Dixmude.

The *Staffel* relocated to the airfield at Wasquehal, on the northeast outskirts of Lille and southeast of Roubaix, on 28 August. The *Flugplatz* at Wasquehal was a well-appointed aerodrome that had been in use since the spring of 1915. A line of sturdy permanent hangars in the southeast corner of the airfield had been cleverly built so as to be camouflaged by adjacent trees. Although Wasquehal was inside the French border, the *Jasta* remained attached to the 4. *Armee*, and it would operate over both Belgium and France.

Strasser's flight log reveals that initially he flew about one sortie per day from Wasquehal in his D V 4408/17. From 3 September onwards he generally flew three patrols a day as the battles over the Ypres salient intensified. Strasser's flight log recorded many flights and encounters with enemy fighters in the weeks to come, but he would not score again until mid-December.

On 7 September replacement pilot Ltn d L Richard Grüter joined the unit. Born on 13 December 1893, he had served with *Grenadier-Regiment* Nr 89 prior to transferring to the air service and being posted to *Jagdstaffel* 17 directly from his training stint at the *Jastaschule* in Valenciennes. Three days after Grüter's arrival the *Staffel* temporarily lost the able services of Günther Schuster when he was transferred to *Jasta* 29. He would score twice more with that unit before returning to *Jasta* 17 in late May 1918 for more success.

At Wasquehal the *Staffel* 17 airmen found themselves opposed by some of the best fighter squadrons that the RFC had. Equipped with the superb SE 5a, the veteran No 60 Sqn had relocated to Ste-Marie-Cappel, just east of St Omer, on 7 September. Its ranks included aces Keith 'Grid' Caldwell and Frank Soden. The celebrated No 56 Sqn, boasting such formidable pilots as James McCudden, Geoffrey Bowman and Gerald Maxwell, was based at nearby Estrée Blanche. Of his opponents, McCudden wrote;

'At this period up on the Ypres sector, the German scout pilots as a rule were undoubtedly good, and one met a larger proportion of skillful pilots up there than I have ever come across on the front from La Fère to the sea. Of course, the Albatros Scout, type D V, was undoubtedly good, but at the same time prisoners said that the German pilots considered the SE 5 a most formidable fighting machine.'

The first adversary to fall to *Jasta* 17 on this new front was another of the vaunted Camels. Early in the morning of 14 September, a flight of Sopwiths from No 70 Sqn was on an offensive patrol to Houthoulst and Roulers. 2Lt E S C Sen, an Indian in the RFC, was flying Camel B2333 when he began to fall behind the rest of his flight with a troublesome engine. Having become separated and disoriented in thick clouds, 2Lt Sen was attacked by four Albatros fighters from *Staffel* 17. At 0750 hrs Vzfw Gustav Schniedewind shot up the Sopwith, which went down losing fuel until it crashed near Menin. 2Lt Sen was lucky to survive as a PoW, and Schniedewind had chalked up his second *Luftsieg*.

16 September was a cloudy day with occasional sunny intervals. Once again the RFC was out in force, resulting in *Jasta* 17 incurring further losses. An early evening patrol, led by the *Staffelführer* Ernst Wendler, attacked the SE 5as of 'A' Flight of No 60 Sqn over Houthem. The scrap was seen by No 56 Sqn's 'B' Flight, led by McCudden, who wrote that he and his men 'dived and attacked the Huns from the rear'.

Another group portrait taken on the steps at Ghistelles has *Jasta* commander Ernst Wendler at front centre (hands on his knees), seated on the knee of Günther Schuster at right. The man to the left of Wendler, hand on hip, is Gustav Schniedewind. Then up the steps in ascending order are Alfred Träger, Adolf Werner, Ehlers, Erich Zschunke, Walter Brachwitz, Julius Buckler, Otto Fitzner, Jakob Wolff, Wilhelm Becker and Georg Strasser (*J Young*)

Ltn d R Alfred Bauer, seen posing with an Albatros D V, was killed during a disastrous combat with elements of Nos 56 and 60 Sqns on 16 September 1917. His Albatros exploded under the fire of Capt Robert L Chidlaw-Roberts of No 60 Sqn. Strasser's logbook entry for that day reads, '*Frontflug. Engagement over enemy lines with numerous Sopwiths (sic). Ltn Bauer has been shot down. Ltn Wendler and Ltn Grüter have to make emergency landings. Ltn Fitzner shoots down a Sopwith*'

Lt Leonard Barlow of No 56 Sqn singled out one of the Albatros D Vs and drove it down, firing both his guns. He saw the machine's propeller stop and the D V went down in a slow righthand spiral. Barlow felt the Albatros was still under control, so he dived and fired again, whereupon the D V went into a zoom. Barlow caught it with another burst and watched it go down near Wervicq. McCudden wrote that he had witnessed Barlow 'finishing off an Albatros in great style', which was confirmed as the 13th of his eventual 20 victories. His victim was either *Jasta* 17 commander Ltn d R Wendler – who was forced to land, wrecking his aircraft – or Richard Grüter, who also crashed his Albatros in the frontlines but escaped unharmed.

The fight did not go entirely the RFC's way, however, as Ltn Otto Fitzner managed to shoot down SE 5a A8909 of No 60 Sqn near Gheluwe for his second combat success. South African 2Lt John Hawtrey was badly wounded and taken prisoner, and he died the next day.

In this same fight the *Staffel* lost Ltn d R Alfred Bauer, killed over Houthem at 1940 hrs. Bauer's Albatros exploded in flames and fell as the second confirmed claim of Capt Robert Leslie Chidlaw-Roberts of No 60 Sqn, who would survive the war with a further nine victories to his name. When interviewed shortly before his death in 1989, Chidlaw-Roberts recalled this success with sincere modesty. Asked if he had achieved any victories, Chidlaw-Roberts responded, 'No, and don't call me an "ace" whatever you do! I recall once firing on an Albatros I think, and it just blew up into little bits. I've never seen it before or since, it nearly made me sick. That was the first one I'd shot down which I really knew I'd got. The ordinary humdrum pilots like me didn't keep a check, unless you were a Ball or a McCudden'.

Strasser was among the *Jasta* 17 pilots participating in the 'catastrophic' fighting of 16 September, his *Flugbuch* entry recording, '*Frontflug. Engagement over enemy lines with numerous Sopwiths. Ltn Bauer has been shot down*'. On this, his third flight of the day, Strasser was unusually flying the Albatros D III formerly used by the recently departed Schuster, the aeroplane being christened *Virginal*. Wendler and Grüter made it back to Wasquehal safely, and the terrible weather conditions of the next two days provided the *Jasta* 17 pilots with some much-needed rest.

The fighting over the Salient soon resumed, however, as the Battle of Menin Road Ridge commenced on the 20th. On 21 September, Gustav Schniedewind was again successful, obtaining credit for a 'Sopwith' east of Ypres at 0821 hrs (at this time many German airmen referred to SE 5a aircraft as 'Sopwiths', the type still being fairly new).

It seems likely that *Jasta* 17 and No 56 Sqn were again involved in the day's action, as a flight of fighters from the latter unit had attacked two-seaters from FAA 227 near Verlinghem Wood. It is possible that *Jasta* 17 became involved, and Schniedewind's claim may refer to the loss of Lt William Potts of No 56 Sqn in SE 5a B4857. However, Potts' comrades reported that his aircraft broke up in the diving attack as he was receiving

defensive fire from the two-seaters. The crew of Ltn Haack and Ltn Klostermann of FAA 227 were also credited with shooting down a 'Sopwith' near Verlinghem Wood. Thus, this may be a case of double credit for one enemy aircraft destroyed.

Julius Buckler returned to *Jagdstaffel* 17 at some date around this period, probably on 21 September. He was apparently fully recovered, and wasted little time. On the evening of the 29th he claimed a 'Sopwith' at Fleurbaix at 1805 hrs for his 14th *Luftsieg*. This actually may refer to an Armstrong-Whitworth FK 8 of No 10 Sqn that had been engaged on an artillery observation mission to Richebourg. The 'Ack-W' was attacked by five enemy scouts and the wounded pilot, Lt E L Burrel, managed to bring it down in British territory. His observer, 2Lt E A Barnard, was unhurt.

On 29 September Strasser recorded his first flight in a Pfalz D III. A few of the sleek, silver-finished fighters had been supplied to the *Jasta* only recently. Unfortunately, the new machine's performance and handling characteristics were proving disappointing, in spite of its good looks.

Buckler was successful again at 1145 hrs on 30 September, claiming another Sopwith in the region of Lens-Arras. That same day, the valuable services of Ltn d R Otto Fitzner were lost to the *Staffel*. Fitzner, who was flying Pfalz D III 1428/17 above Wasquehal airfield possibly on a test flight, suddenly went into a spin from an altitude of about 200-300 metres and crashed heavily onto the aerodrome. He was hospitalised for a month.

The month of October did not start auspiciously. *Jasta* 17's third *Staffelführer* Ernst Wendler was reportedly wounded in action and then crashed, sustaining a concussion (most accounts have him being wounded on 1 October, but he may not have left the unit until the 8th). Having recovered, Wendler would eventually complete two undistinguished terms as commander of home-defence *Kampfeinsitzer-Staffel* (Kest) formations.

The crash of Pfalz D III 1428/17 sidelined the budding ace Ltn d R Otto Fitzner on 30 September 1917. Fitzner spun in from a height of between 200 and 300 metres, crashing on the aerodrome at Wasquehal. He was out of action for a month

The buckled fuselage of Pfalz D III 1428/17 bears witness to the impact that injured Otto Fitzner on 30 September. Fitzner would return to *Jasta* 17 on 30 October and claim one more victory with the unit before leaving to command *Jasta* 65 in March 1918 (*E Lambrecht*)

This wonderful view captures *Jasta* 17 under the command of Hptm Rudolf *Freiherr* von Esebeck, who took command on 4 October and was held in high esteem by all *Staffel* personnel. On the left, from bottom to top, are von Esebeck, Ltn Wilhelm Becker, Ltn Alfred Träger, Ltn d L Richard Grüter, and Vzfw Gustav Schniedewind. On the right, again from bottom to top, are Buckler's old observer Oblt Hubertus *Freiherr* von Rudno-Rudzinski, Ltn d R Walter Brachwitz, Vzfw Brendel, Vzfw Adolf Schreder and Buckler

It was not long before Wendler's replacement arrived. Hptm Rudolf *Freiherr* von Esebeck would be remembered with great respect and fondness by all *Jasta* 17 men who flew under his command. Born in Karlsruhe on 8 March 1888, von Esebeck had served in the *Garde-Regiment zu Fuss* Nr 2. It is believed that he was flying with *Flieger-Abteilung* 15 as early as September 1915. December 1916 found him serving as a fighter pilot with *Jasta* 8, and it was in that unit that he downed an FE 2d of No 20 Sqn on 6 February 1917. From *Jasta* 8 the nobleman was posted to *Kest* 7 as its commander on 12 June 1917, then on to *Jasta* 17.

On 5 October Julius Buckler joyfully welcomed his old observer Oblt *Freiherr* von Rudno-Rudzinski to the *Staffel*. 'Rudno' had completed his pilot training and would fly with *Jasta* 17 for two months. He would not score any victories prior to being being posted to command *Jasta* 60 in January 1918, however.

During October other pilots like Strasser were certainly engaging the enemy, but only Buckler succeeded in getting confirmed victories. Strasser recorded inconclusive fights in his D V 4408/17 on the 5th and 7th, when he engaged a Nieuport. On 11 October – a day of low clouds and rain – Buckler tallied his first 'double' of the war. At 0945 hrs he led two other *Jasta* 17 pilots in an attack on an RE 8 over Roclincourt. The crew from No 5 Sqn, Lts F C E Clarke (pilot) and P Mighell, were both badly wounded by Buckler's unerring fire and the RE 8 was forced to land south of Farbus. Clarke died of his wounds later that day, and Mighell shared the same fate on the 12th.

Buckler was hardly finished for the day, and at 1620 hrs he pounced on the struggling Camel B6324 flown by 2Lt W H Winter of No 28 Sqn. According to Winter's later statement, he was on formation flying practice in one of the unit's newly-issued Camels when he lost the group and strayed east of the lines. Forced to descend by mist, he was then fired on by German flak – and apparently Buckler – before coming down southwest of Lille to be taken prisoner. In less than two weeks since his return to this hotly contested Front, Buckler had raised his score from 13 to 17 victories. His good friend Georg Strasser, meanwhile, went on leave from 16 October to 3 November.

Vzfw Buckler kept up the pressure on the RFC six days later, shooting up a Bristol F 2B from No 11 Sqn on 17 October. The ill-fated crew of 2Lt S E Stanley and his observer Lt E L Fosse were on a photographic reconnaissance mission when they suffered engine trouble. Buckler was again leading a *Kette* of three machines when he attacked the Bristol Fighter over Recourt at 1020 hrs. The aeroplane was last seen by British observers in a vertical dive over Sensée. Pilot Stanley had been shot in the chest, and in the subsequent crash observer Fosse was injured in the arm and taken prisoner. He was luckier than Stanley, however, who died of his wounds two days later.

On 24 October the weather cleared up and plenty of aerial combat ensued. Buckler once again found an RE 8 (from No 16 Sqn) out on an artillery-spotting mission over Méricourt at 0320 hrs. The pilot, Lt A O Balaam, and his observer, 2Lt D Prince-Smith, put up the best fight they could, but against a foe of Buckler's calibre they had little chance. The doomed RE 8 (B5896) was hit hard and spun down out of control to 180 metres, at which point it nose-dived in flames into the sodden ground – both men were killed.

Finally, three days later, a different *Jasta* 17 pilot put his name in the October logbook. On the 27th Ltn d R Brachwitz succeeded in claiming a Sopwith single-seater south of Méricourt at 1235 hrs. This may well have been one of three Camels from No 43 Sqn that were shot up that morning, resulting in the deaths of two pilots.

Buckler did not rest on his laurels, for with his score nearing 20, high honours and decorations were in the offing. Another of the hapless artillery-spotting RE 8s fell to his lethal fire on 28 October. He found the two-seater over Mont St Eloi and pounced at about 1605 hrs. The crew of Lt E H Keir (pilot) and Capt C W C Casey both perished in the fiery crash. Buckler's score now stood at 20, but he was still an NCO – high Prussian decorations such as the *Hohenzollern* and the *Pour le Mérite* were only awarded to officers.

The next day (the 29th) Buckler returned to the job of balloon-busting, targeting a British 'gasbag' at Neuville. He succeeded in setting it ablaze at 0914 hrs, but he was only getting started. About three hours later he was credited with an aircraft downed east of Houthem at 1210 hrs. Nieuport 27 B3630 of No 1 Sqn RFC, flown by 2Lt A W McLaughlin, was last seen going down with seven enemy fighters on its tail – McLaughlin was killed. This was Buckler's second double.

The morning of 30 October saw the resumption of the British ground offensive, with the village of Passchendaele as its objective. The next day broke with bright and clear skies, and the intensity of the fighting in the air matched the ferocity of the muddy struggle that was taking place on the ground.

Vzfw Georg Strasser poses with an Albatros D V in this fine view, which was used as the basis for one of the famous Sanke postcards, Number 638. Strasser recorded unsuccessful combats in his D V 4408/17 on 5 and 7 October (*L Bronnenkant*)

Buckler's Albatros D V forms the centrepiece for this view of *Jasta* 17 groundcrewmen at Wasquehal airfield. Buckler's usual *Mops* legend was painted in white on a two-colour fuselage band, and the machine also bore the usual black tail of the *Staffel*. Buckler was a veritable juggernaut in October 1917, achieving nine victories. His first mechanic, Uffz Roth, is no doubt among this group. Buckler wrote that he was 'a first-class engine specialist and extremely skilled rigger' who always tuned whatever machine Buckler received until it was the fastest machine in the *Staffel*

Buckler takes a relaxed pose by his *Mops* Albatros D V with the black tail. The propeller bears the trademark of the Astra firm. Buckler had brought his tally to 20 by 28 October, and he would score four more times before the month was out. His best day, however, would come with his 'hat trick' performed on 18 November

Buckler put in a claim for another 'RE', but he may have been mistaken in his identification. An Armstrong-Whitworth FK 8 of No 10 Sqn was out on a photographic mission that morning, and it is likely that its crew of 2Lt W Davidson (pilot) and Canadian observer Lt W Crowther were the ones who had the misfortune to encounter Buckler. They went down in flames north of La Basée, both of the crewmen perishing.

As October 1917 closed, the personnel of *Jasta* 17 may have reflected on their most successful month of the war so far. The entire *Staffel* had recorded 146 aerial combats in October and been credited with ten victories. *Draufgänger* Buckler had scored no fewer than nine of them, with the tenth success being claimed by Brachwitz. Wasenmüller's accounting states that the *Staffel* pilots made 296 'front flights' in spite of the weather, and logged 286.5 hours of *Staffel* flying.

1 November was another day in the monotonous round of rain, fog and low clouds. The weather did not improve over the next eight days, severely limiting the aerial action on both sides of the quagmire that constituted the frontlines. On the 6th the weather cleared enough for the *Jasta* 17 pilots to fly to their new airfield at Erkeghem (or Erkegem), near Oostkamp. They had returned to Belgium and remained attached to the German 4. *Armee*, but their stay here would last just two weeks. Georg Strasser flew his Albatros D V 4408/17 on at least 12 frontline patrols from Erkegem, but once again it was Buckler who took the limelight.

The unit's leading ace baptised the new aerodrome on 12 November when he claimed yet another RE near Oostkerke at 1545 hrs. He may have shot up an aircraft of No 6 Sqn, as one of its RE 8s returned with 2AM G Wyatt wounded. At any rate, Buckler had obtained his 25th confirmed victory, and this success finally gained him some recognition. On the same 12 November his Golden Military Merit Cross was approved in Berlin. This was commonly referred to as the '*Pour le Mérite* for the Little Man', the latter term referring to someone from the ranks, and not an officer. Buckler was only the fourth member of the air service to have received this decoration by November 1917. He would go on to become the first of just five aces who received the Golden Military Merit Cross and, after being promoted, earned the *Pour le Mérite* too.

One week earlier, on 5 November, Buckler had received the Hessian Warrior's Honour Decoration in Iron.

The unrelenting aerial combat continued, with Strasser recording a few inconclusive fights in D V 4408/17, plus one flight in a Pfalz, on the 13th. Two days later there was an intense series of engagements fought by the *Jasta*, with Buckler finding another of his favourite artillery-spotting targets northeast of Ypres at 0845 hrs. This time, RE 8 A4652 of No 21 Sqn, flown by 2Lt W A Barnett with observer Lt G J Bakewell, was forced to crash-land. Both of RFC crewmen died of their injuries. In spite of Buckler's 26th victory there was probably little celebration in the *Jasta* mess that evening, for British bombers had struck the *Staffel* airfield earlier in the day. Ltn d R Ehlers was badly wounded in the right leg during the attack, resulting in him leaving the unit.

Rain and foggy conditions persisted over the next six days, but flying by both sides was taken up again on the 18th, in spite of the notorious 'Flanders Fog'. 'On 18 November thick fog lay over the entire Flanders Front', wrote Buckler. 'Three days earlier I had shot down my 26th opponent.

'As usual, I was first at breakfast in the morning. In the prevailing fog an operational flight was unthinkable. All the tents were closed – only mine stood open. My machine's motor had just been overhauled and was being test-run. It was running so smoothly that I was itching to open it wide.

Comrades in arms. The deep friendship between Julius Buckler (on the left, with his favourite stocking cap) and Georg Strasser is evident from this view, most likely taken at Wasquehal. Although he flew many patrols in October and November, Strasser would not score again until December, when he downed two balloons in rapid succession

In a few minutes I was in the air and flying an extended circuit around the airfield, although I could not fly higher than 100 metres, but at this height the visibility was relatively good.

'Why not take a little trip to the front? When I was about five kilometres from the front I saw an enemy balloon floating over Zillebeke Lake. The number "27" popped into my head. The balloon was hanging at a distance of about ten kilometres from me, so with a speed of about 160 kilometres per hour, I needed just a few minutes to reach it. I tested my guns then I plunged into the mist.

'Those few minutes of blind flying seemed so awfully long to me at that time that I left the "pea soup" again four times in order to be breathe freely for a moment. When those minutes passed the balloon was still hanging far behind the enemy lines – I had underestimated the distance. I sped directly toward it at a height of about 50 metres. They were hauling it down as I opened fire and it burned. In the same minute, three enemy aircraft came to greet me. In addition, the guns on the ground were firing everything they had at me, but the "soup" was my salvation as it cut me off from view.

'Now, as I chased through the grey mist I no longer had any idea where I was. Without a compass and without the aid of the sun, I had no reference indicating in which direction I should fly. So trusting in my star, I flew on haphazardly in some sort of direction, and after a few minutes spotted an airfield below me. I throttled back and began to glide.

'What's this? Enemy aircraft in the air beside me! Enemy aircraft below me on the airfield! I had the engine at full throttle and yanked the joystick into my belly, again disappearing into the "soup". When I came back out of the muck again after a few minutes I saw an enemy observation balloon below me! I quickly surveyed the situation. Below me lay Dickebusch, so my home was over there. This "gasbag" had served for a long time directing fire into our trenches, so at full speed I pounced on it, although it was already going down in a hurry. After a few moments it was ablaze, its observer hanging peacefully from a parachute and swinging to and fro.

'I did not wait for a parting "blessing" from below, but rather swiftly took to my heels or, more accurately, to the mists from whence I came.'

Buckler's first balloon, claimed at 1910 hrs near Ypres, was from the British 36th Section, 17th Company, 2nd Balloon Wing. The second one, at Dickebusch, was timed at 0925 hrs. Buckler went on to state that he landed at the Boistrancourt aerodrome of the Flashar *Staffel*, or *Jasta* 5. After refuelling he flew back to Erkeghem, where he attempted to keep his two victories a secret for a while;

'When I landed everyone was assembled on the field feeling nervous. Some had already feared the worst but now everyone revealed themselves to be very glad that I was back again. The good *Freiherr* von Esebeck suggested that we head as quickly as possible to the officers' mess for breakfast.

'I acted tired and taciturn, although I found it difficult to remain silent about the two victories. Fortunately, right after soup, a report came to my aid stating that there was lively aerial activity to be observed at the front. [*Staffelführer*] von Esebeck asked, "Buckler, what do you think? Should we eat first or should we take off immediately?" I quickly responded, "Take off!"

'Perhaps the report had been transmitted late, as when we arrived at the front there was practically nothing going on. I gave the signal to split up, which meant that everyone could do what he wanted to. About ten kilometres behind enemy lines I spotted an RE, which I selected as my 29th. The cloud layer hung at about 600 metres and was fairly solid. Using it as cover, I flew towards the enemy. During the duel that ensued I forced

Ltn Alfred Träger is seen with his Albatros D V named *'Sonnenvogel'* (sunbird), emblazoned with a sunburst emblem. In the raucous celebrations accompanying Buckler's triple victory of 18 November and his promotion to leutnant, Träger is said to have ridden a bicycle through the rooms of the pilots' quarters, bruising himself considerably

him down to 30 metres, then victory was mine. He caught fire and crashed.'

According to RFC records, the crew of RE 8 A3669 from No 9 Sqn was out on yet another dangerous, but vital, artillery observation mission and reported that they had been attacked by five enemy aircraft. The RE's fuel tank was hit and the pilot, 2Lt W Courtis, succeeded in bringing the aircraft safely down in British lines near Langemarck. The crew reported that Buckler and the other *Staffel* 17 pilots flew down to low level in their attack. The observer, 2Lt E T Taylor, continued to fire his Lewis Gun at them after the RE 8 was on the ground. The crew exited their machine safely, but it was soon destroyed by German artillery.

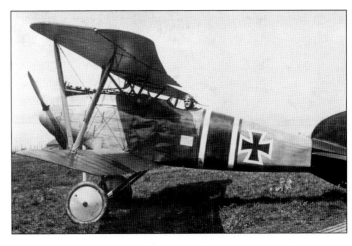

Ltn Alfred Träger would score no confirmed victories, but he was a popular and reliable comrade and his name often turns up in Buckler's memoir. According to the latter, Träger's sheepdog 'Greif' had such sharp hearing that he could detect the approach of enemy aircraft long before any listening post. Träger's OAW-built Albatros D III 1694/17 displayed the unit's black tail insignia, as well as the familiar Iron Cross ribbon band marking on the fuselage

Returning to Buckler's narrative;

'I had no time to flee back into the clouds so I allowed the hell-fire that broke out from the earth to pass over me and flew at full throttle towards my own lines. Gunfire crackled from all sides, but as long as the engine and I remained intact, it was all the same to me. Then I suddenly saw an aircraft appear close behind me, which I thought was an enemy. Cursing, I braced myself for a new battle, but when I took a closer look I recognised von Rudno, my old observer. The faithful soul had stuck with me during the entire flight.

'When I announced to von Esebeck, "Offz-Stv Buckler reports the downing of two observation balloons and an RE", there was a great hullabaloo.'

Exhausted by the morning's actions, Buckler took a nap. Later that afternoon he received a telephone call from *Kogenluft* (General in Command of the Army Air Service) himself, his Excellency Gen Ernst von Hoeppner. According to Buckler, von Hoeppner personally congratulated him on his three victories and his promotion to leutnant der reserve! Finally, Buckler had achieved his long-desired appointment as an officer 'based on my own flying ability, not a certificate or exam'. That evening, von Esebeck led the entire *Staffel* in a very wet and festive celebration honouring Buckler for his triple victory, and his promotion. 'I got to see Alfred Träger mount a bicycle and ride through four rooms, during which he ran into every edge and corner and scratched himself badly', wrote Buckler of the night's party. 'Then he knocked me down. While my comrades were celebrating in my honour I was already lying in my bed by 11 o'clock'.

There was no relief from the daily action, however. On the 19th Buckler was forced to land after an unsuccessful combat. The following day the *Jasta* received orders to leave Belgium and the Flanders Front, as the famous 'Tank Battle of Cambrai' had erupted to the south on the German 2. *Armee* Front. Supported by large numbers of tanks, and without the typical advance warning of a long pre-battle bombardment, the British Third Army had penetrated the German lines to a depth of 10,000 yards. There was only one *Jasta* in the 2. *Armee,* and *Jasta* 17 was just one of several German aviation units rushed to the area.

CAMBRAI AND BEYOND

On 20 November 1917 *Jasta* 17 was directed to proceed to an airfield at Neuvilly, near Le Cateau, to reinforce the threatened 2. *Armee* Front under the command of *General der Kavallerie* Georg von der Marwitz. *Jasta* 8 would join it there, and the two would share the airfield. These two *Staffeln*, along with Bavarian *Jasta* 35, would compose *Jagdgruppe* 2. According to Buckler;

'We received the order to move immediately to the vicinity of Cambrai. Due to low-lying mist we took off at three-minute intervals. Two hours later we had all landed smoothly at the new airfield assigned to us. Towards evening, with improving visibility, we also undertook an exploratory flight. We used the two foggy days that followed our arrival to have the machines examined and the engines overhauled. We had to be fully prepared to engage in the counter-offensive that was to take place on 30 November. We had difficult tasks ahead of us.

'In spite of the bad weather I wandered along the front alone on 29 November. In the vicinity of Bapaume I spotted a balloon about 12 kilometres behind the enemy lines. The cloud ceiling hung down to about 200 metres, so there could not have been more favourable weather for an attack on a balloon. However, it seemed to me that the approaching flight was taking forever, and as so often happens it took some effort to overcome my inner agitation.

'I wondered whether the balloon observer still had no idea what was in store for him. It was now high time for him to bail out! However, this time I was the one who was surprised, as I had never before seen an observer remain calmly in his basket greeting me with machine gun fire. I was so shocked that at first I thought an enemy aircraft had made a sneak attack on me from behind. I turned aside, but saw nothing. I only heard something smack into *Mops*, after which I immediately turned again towards the balloon.

'Now I noticed that the observer was the brave machine gunner. I now hammered furiously away at the "gasbag", and also aimed my machine guns at the man in the basket. Fortunately, I did not hit him, and the brave man was able to use his parachute at just the right moment before the balloon caught fire.'

This 30th confirmed victory for Buckler was a balloon from the British Section 31, 18th Company, 3rd Balloon Wing, which went ablaze at 1104 hrs. Unbeknownst to Buckler there were two observers in the basket – Lts Weeks and Goodwin – and both men survived his attack. That evening Buckler wrote, 'We were ordered to Le Cateau, where a long discussion took place concerning the deployment of our *Staffel* for the next day – the day of the attack'.

30 November was indeed the day planned for the highly successful German counter-attack at Cambrai – a total tactical surprise that would

Buckler poses with one of his Albatros D V fighters, bearing the black tail of *Jasta* 17. Alhough a flare cartridge rack has been fitted to the side of the cockpit, the D V does not seem to display Buckler's usual *Mops* legend. He scored his 30th victory on 29 November 1917

quickly retake much of the ground that had been lost in the British assault of ten days earlier. That night everyone in *Jasta* 17 went to bed early, as they were scheduled for an early takeoff in order to rendezvous with other units by 0830 hrs. If we are to believe his highly dramatic account, Buckler spent a restless night troubled by foreboding dreams of being wounded yet again. In the morning he told his orderly, Meisenbach, 'Today I'm going to catch it!'

The scheduled units succeeded in meeting at their assigned locations. Each German artillery-ranging two-seater was to be escorted by two Albatros fighters from *Jasta* 17. Because they were short a man, Buckler took on the escorting duties for one of the two-seaters alone;

'The outward and return flights went smoothly the first two times. During the third approach, I thought to myself that if the English were smart they would cut us off this time. Below me I saw two Sopwiths, but before attacking them I took the precaution of looking to the right and left. I did so too late.

'From the left an enemy pilot was charging my flank, being less than ten metres from me. His machine guns, hammering wildly at me, could not miss their mark. I experienced a blow to my back and felt both of my arms get hit. Before they dropped down limp and useless, I was able to push the control column into the corner and kept it there with my right foot. My machine turned vertically around its own axis, with the ground approaching at a furious speed. Mustering all of my strength, I succeeded in turning off the ignition at the last moment before the machine crashed in the middle of a field of craters. When I was able to survey the situation I was hanging upside down staring into a shell hole. Despite tremendous pain, I loosened my belt and let myself fall.'

The many successes of Buckler and others of the *Jasta* would not have been possible without the work of the groundcrews. *Jasta* 17 boasted some very clever mechanics indeed. This unique Albatros D V in *Jasta* 17 markings has had the spinner removed and a rounded nose (similar to those seen on some Austro-Hungarian Oeffag-built D IIIs) fitted. The spinners sometimes came loose during flight, thus the reason for what is believed to be a frontline modification. This D V also displayed the new unit marking of a white fin and aft fuselage, with a black rudder and tailplane, instituted around the end of 1917 (*1914 Aviation Heritage Trust*)

There is a possibility that Buckler had fallen to a member of No 56 Sqn, which had moved to Laviéville on 12 November. Geoffrey Hilton Bowman was the leader of 'C' Flight with a current score of 21 (out of an eventual 32). He reported attacking an Albatros V-strutter that went down south of Bantouzelle – this is very close to the known location of Buckler's crash near Vaucelles, south of Cambrai near the St Quentin Canal.

Buckler's situation was dire, for he had fallen in no-man's land between the lines;

'My machine lay on its back, with broken wings on the sloped side of a shell hole partially sticking out of it. Fuel was dripping on my head from above. I lay in my hole cringing like an animal that someone had wounded in its burrow. If someone did not find me soon I would have to perish here. I heard bullets whistling over my shell hole and shells were impacting all around me.'

Luckily for Buckler, he lay in the zone of the German counter-attack. He stayed in the shell hole for many hours before advancing German medical orderlies found him and gingerly carried him on a sheet to a casualty clearing station.

'Three hours later von Esebeck, Rudno and our faithful Uffz Koch were at my bedside in order to pick me up with the largest car of the *Staffel*. Rudno had also brought along champagne and cigarettes. The stretcher was laid across the car, and as carefully as possible it set off on its way to Le Cateau. Brachwitz, one of our comrades, had already brought home the report that he had seen my aircraft lying shot down between the lines, and they had little hope of seeing me alive again.'

Buckler was soon undergoing an operation in Le Cateau. His arms were so badly wounded that there was concern for some weeks that he would lose one or both of them.

At the front, meanwhile, Vzfw Schniedewind did his best to make up for Buckler's absence. On 1 December he claimed an 'RE' over Noble Ville at 1350 hrs. This may well have been another misidentified Armstrong-Whitworth FK 8, this time from No 35 Sqn. FK 8 B5778 was

Another view of the round-nose *Jasta* 17 D V reveals the personal insignia of coloured fuselage bands. The D V next to it displays the colours of *Jasta* 12. Unfortunately, no other information on this interesting machine is available (*1914 Aviation Heritage Trust*)

on a contact patrol to the vicinity of Villers Guislain when it went missing – pilot Lt J MacKenzie and observer 2Lt C Hyde were both killed. Unfortunately, this victory was offset that same day by the wounding of Walter Brachwitz in the thigh – he had possibly been shot down by Australian DH 5 pilots of No 68 Sqn. He died of his wound in the same hospital room as Buckler after lingering until 23 December.

POUR LE MÉRITE

Buckler's situation was still in doubt on 3 December. If we are to believe the ace's story, that day a nurse came and tidied up the room, making sure the patient was presentable for important visitors. Then a hauptmann entered, and in a low, gentle voice he prepared Buckler for what was to come. Presently, 'A general with a snow-white moustache entered. It was Gen von der Marwitz'. The commander-in-chief of the entire 2. *Armee* sat down besides Buckler's bed and surprised the incredulous young airman by relating some details of his life in a fatherly manner. He had always been a soldier, and had won the *Pour le Mérite mit Eichenlaub*. The white-haired general said he had accepted the medal, 'Not for me, but for my troops. But how wonderful it must be for the young ones to receive such an Order entirely for their own accomplishments'.

After that, the old gentleman took out a small black case, removed the blue and gold cross of the Order and placed the ribbon around the terribly injured flier's neck. Still heavily sedated, Buckler drifted off to merciful sleep with the General grasping the fingers of his hand that protruded from out of the plaster cast. Little wonder that Buckler recalled, 'When I woke up again three hours later I felt around for the cross on my neck in order to convince myself that the whole thing had not been a dream'.

Buckler's recovery would take months. His hospital room in Le Cateau was visited daily by his *Jasta* 17 friends. Buckler was transferred on 23 December to a private hospice in Mainz, where he continued his long recuperation. It was not until eight weeks after the

Julius Buckler is seen after his promotion to leutnant and his award of the *Pour le Mérite* in this fine portrait. In his book, Buckler claimed that he had been promoted to Active Army leutnant in *Flieger-Bataillon* Nr 1. This would have been quite unusual, and most records indicate that Buckler was promoted to leutnant der reserve, and not an active officer in the Regular Army. His 'Blue Max' was awarded to him during his hospital stay, on 3 December 1917 (*L Bronnenkant*)

Vzfw Brendel of *Jasta* 17 poses with his Albatros D Va in a photograph possibly taken on Rethéuil Ferme aerodrome. The fighter displays the new *Staffel* marking of a white fin and aft fuselage, with a black rudder and (usually) tailplane, instituted around the end of 1917. Brendel's D Va was individually identified by diagonal stripes on the fuselage, probably in light blue

Georg Strasser is seen with his Albatros D V (probably 4408/17) named *Ly*, emblazoned with a heart emblem and tasteful black and white décor. Strasser flamed two balloons in December 1917 to bring his tally to seven. Although he would make many more flights in January and February 1918, he would not score again

operation that his right arm cast could be removed. His left arm, with its severed artery, required another operation, and he was finally allowed to stand two weeks after that.

By that time *Jasta* 17 had been relocated to another airfield in the 2. *Armee*, the unit moving to Rethéuil Ferme, near Bohain, on 7 December. Karl Wasenmüller's photo albums contain shots of a line of the unit's tent hangars on the snowy airfield at Rethéuil Ferme, with the caption '*Zirkus Esebeck*' – a nickname for the unit derived from its circus-like tent accommodations.

Also on the 7th, the *Staffel* lost another of its best pilots when Vzfw Gustav Schniedewind was transferred to *Jasta* I (F) in distant Palestine. There, he would bring his tally to seven, before being badly wounded on 23 May 1918. Returning to Germany, he received his own Military Merit Cross on 28 May. Schniedewind would recover and finish the war in FA 305.

Worsening winter weather began to limit flying opportunities even more, but on 10 December Georg Strasser could finally record another victory in his *Flugbuch*. Flying his usual Albatros D V 4408/17, at 1545 hrs he flamed a French observation balloon near Jussy, south of St Quentin. The balloon from the 92*e Cié des Aerostiers* was his sixth confirmed claim. Two days later he repeated this feat, but this time against a British balloon of the 29th Kite Balloon, 14th Company, 3rd Wing at Villers Faucon. The observer, 2Lt B Thomas was wounded in the attack. This was the seventh, and final, victory that the reliable Württemberger would achieve.

The second December of the war for *Jasta* 17 had once again brought a lull in aerial action, but the *Staffel* still recorded 97 front flights that month. On 28 December the *Staffel* became a component of *Jagdgruppe* 1, which also consisted of *Jagdstaffeln* 8, 24 and 48 under the command of Hptm von Bentheim. Its affiliation also changed from the 2. *Armee* to the newly formed 18. *Armee*. In exchange for the three victories in December,

the *Staffel* mourned the losses of Brachwitz and Ltn Stanislaus Zentsytzki, the latter pilot being killed on the airfield in the crash of a two-seater he was flying on the 18th. The flying tapered off in the last weeks of December, bringing 1917 to an uneventful end.

Ltn Alfred Träger strikes an informal pose on a snowy airfield with his Albatros D Va, which was reportedly named *'Adler'* (Eagle). It was emblazoned with a beautiful stylised eagle emblem on the fuselage, and the new unit markings of a black and white tail

1918

The final year of the war did not start out impressively for *Jasta* 17. The *Staffel* had temporarily lost the talented services of Buckler, and Schniedewind was off to Palestine. On the 5th Buckler's friend Oblt Rudno-Rudzinski left to take command of the new *Jasta* 60. Whether due to these losses, the winter weather or the lack of aerial opposition, not one confirmed victory for *Jasta* 17 was scored from 1 January to 5 March 1918. On the other hand, there were no recorded casualties either. The Battle of Cambrai was the last ground offensive until the spring of 1918, and aerial activity slackened off on both sides.

The pilots were still braving the winter weather and patrols were still being flown. Karl Wasenmüller's accounts for 1918 are limited, but he did record that the *Staffel* collectively made 120 front flights in January 1918. Strasser's flight log reveals that from 1 January to 11 February, he made 28 flights. Most of these were in his trusted D V 4408/17, except for a flight in a Pfalz on 29 January and an alternate Albatros (identified only by the letter 'B' on its fuselage) on 13 January. On the 14th Ltn d R Otto Fitzner left on sick leave and would not return until 5 March. His talents would be missed.

One bright note in January was the arrival of the experienced Ltn d R Karl Bohny from *Kest* 7 on the 18th. Bohny had served briefly with *Jasta* 5 in early 1917, before being posted to *Kest* 7, where he claimed two victories. He would stay with *Jasta* 17 for the rest of the war (with the exception of a period of sick leave in February) and down six more confirmed adversaries.

Inexplicably, Georg Strasser's flight log record ends abruptly on 11 February 1918. According to French historians Yves Bailleux and Christophe Cony, there is an obscure note among Strasser's records that indicate he was briefly transferred to *Jasta* 9 at Leffincourt from 21 to 25 February, but then returned to *Jasta* 17. There is no confirmed explanation, but it is also suggested there may have been tension between Strasser and Hptm von Esebeck, based on a letter Strasser wrote. By 18 March 1918 Strasser was in the hospital at Maubege, and from there

One of the more spectacular Albatros D Vs in *Jasta* 17 was this one named *Gisi* (a nickname for Giselle). The name was woven into a lightning bolt, which blazed from a black thundercloud. The pilot seen here is Oblt Hubertus *Freiherr* von Rudno-Rudzinski, who left *Jagdstaffel* 17 for leadership of *Jasta* 60 in January 1918. He would not be the only pilot photographed in *Gisi*, however

This photograph provides a broader view of the elaborately decorated *Gisi* D V. It too displayed the new *Staffel* marking of a black and white tail. An unidentified mechanic is in the cockpit

he was transferred to Brieg, in Germany. The cause of his hospitalisation remains unknown, but he seems to have eventually returned to *Jasta* 17. Indeed, a group photograph shows that Strasser was still with the unit apparently as late as mid-May 1918. At some unknown time soon after this he left the unit for FEA 5, where his technical knowledge and experience could be put to good use.

Wasenmüller's accounting states that the *Jasta* made 111 front flights in February 1918. Although no victories were recorded, the pilots were no doubt looking forward to better weather, and anticipating the action that would accompany Ludendorff's great spring offensive. The decision had been made to launch an offensive along the line from Arras to La Fère in an attempt to break through toward Amiens – before the weight of American manpower and industry could be brought to bear. This massive operation would be aptly named the *Kaiserschlacht*, or Imperial Battle, by Gen Erich Ludendorff. It was scheduled to begin on 21 March.

As the aerial activity increased in March, *Jasta* 17 could finally add another triumph to its list. On the 5th Offz Stv Adolf Schreder, who had previously marked his Albatros D V with a red blitz insignia, shot down a SE 5a. It was very likely B145 of No 24 Sqn, which crashed southeast of Vendhuille at 1500 hrs. 2Lt W F Poulter was on an offensive patrol and was last seen by his squadronmates getting shot up near Villers Outréaux. Badly wounded, he came down in German territory and died the following day. This was Adolf Schreder's first confirmed victory, but his glory would be short-lived.

If Buckler's memoirs are correct, he was finally able to return to *Jasta* 17 on 4 March 1918. Now he was Ltn d R Buckler with the *Pour le Mérite* glistening at his throat. He returned via the familiar airfield at Metz-Frescaty, and found that 'My *Staffel* mate [Karl] Bohny, "Little Bohny" we called him, had come to Metz to pick me up in a touring aircraft'. The flight to the *Jasta* airfield was unnerving for Buckler, as he was a helpless passenger subjected to what he referred to as Bohny's wild and 'God-awful' flying technique.

'During the 12 weeks in which I had been away from the front a lot had changed', wrote Buckler. 'Now formations of 20 to 30 [enemy] bombers attacked the rear areas by night. My comrades told me that the "good old times" at the front were pretty much over. The French and English were flying in larger and larger formations'. Buckler was now the most successful pilot in the *Staffel* by far, and he recorded that he generally led the unit in the air, although von Esebeck was the actual

Offz Stv Adolf Schreder decorated his Albatros D V with a striking 'blitz' emblem on the fuselage, presumably in red with a thin black border. He claimed his first, and only, victory on 5 March 1918

commander. Buckler had two machines at his disposal – his usual *Mops*, and one named *Lilly*.

Having also returned from his sick leave on 5 March, Ltn d R Otto Fitzner wasted little time in getting to grips with the enemy once again. On the 8th he shot up a French Breguet 14 bomber near Tilloy Ferme at 1215 hrs for his third victory. The Breguets were formidable opponents, being well armed and capable of taking considerable punishment. That same day, Ltn Wilhelm Becker crashed Albatros D V 2231/17 on the *Staffel* airfield near Bohain – the aeroplane went up in flames and Becker was slightly injured.

On 16 March, as part of the reorganisation of units in preparation for the German spring offensive, *Jasta* 17 was named a component *Staffel* of *Jagdgruppe* 2 (*Jagdstaffeln* 17, 22, and 63). This *Gruppe* would be commanded by *Jasta* 17's own leader, Hptm Rudolf von Esebeck. The *Staffel* remained based at Rethéuil Ferme, near Bohain, in the 18. *Armee*.

The rising spirits of the *Jasta* 17 pilots were dampened on 17 March, however. Just 12 days after his first confirmed victory, Adolf Schreder was killed in action four kilometres west of Busigny, not far from Bohain, at 1150 hrs. He was reportedly flying one of the unit's Pfalz fighters at the time, but there is little else known about his demise.

Karl Bohny was posted to *Jasta* 17 on 18 January 1918, where he would claim the final six of his eight victories. He flew Julius Buckler back to *Jasta* 17 on 4 March 1918 following Buckler's convalescence from his wounds of 30 November 1917 (*N Franks*)

On 17 March 1918 Adolf Schreder was killed in action. He is seen here with his Albatros D V decorated with his 'blitz' insignia

The location of this interesting group of *Jasta* 17 Albatros fighters is unconfirmed, but it may have been Douilly airfield. The unit's stay at Douilly only lasted from 26 to 28 March 1918. The aircraft marked with a 'B' may have been flown once by Strasser, according to his flight log. The D Va at right with the chequered markings was the machine of von Esebeck. It displayed his family's crest shield of two roses on a dark blue field (top) and one rose against a light yellow field (bottom). The chequerboard band was probably blue and yellow as well (*1914 Aviation Heritage Trust*)

KAISERSCHLACHT

On 21 March 1918, what many Germans simply called the *Grosse Schlacht in Frankreich* erupted on the fronts of three German Armies. As part of *General der Infanterie* Oskar von Hutier's 18. *Armee, Jasta* 17 would play its role in what Wasenmüller called the 'Breakthrough Battle at St Quentin-La Fére'. On 21 March there was little flying possible until midday due to the poor weather. On the 22nd the *Jagdstaffeln* carried out escort flights for infantry-contact aircraft flying at an altitude of 500 metres. Strong formations of French aircraft attacked from the south to support the British.

On 28 March Karl Bohny contributed his share to the offensive efforts when he downed a two-seater at 1425 hrs at Marquevillers. It is possible that Bohny's victim was British Armstrong Whitworth FK 8 C8456 of No 82 Sqn, crewed by 2Lts T Watson and T Taylor, both of whom were killed.

As the German infantry assaults gained ground, the air units had to advance to keep up with the troops. On 26 March *Jasta* 17 moved to an airfield at Douilly, but the time spent there was brief indeed. Two days later the *Staffel* moved to the large ex-French airfield at Balâtre, which soon became home to approximately 150 German aircraft. The fighters of *Jagdgeschwader* II occupied the aerodrome at the same time. Such a large number of machines did not escape the notice of the enemy, and the airfield would soon be targeted by Allied bombers.

1 April brought both triumph and tragedy to *Jagdstaffel* 17. Ltn Wilhelm Becker was credited with downing a French two-seater recorded as an 'AR 2' near Mesnil at 0840 hrs. However, the same day Ltn d L Richard Grüter was killed in action near Montdidier. He was *Jasta* 17's first casualty of the offensive.

During this period a flier arrived who would play an important role in the battles to come. Ltn d R Alfred Fleischer was posted in on 12 April 1918. He had become enchanted with aviation at the age of 18 when he witnessed the famous French aerobatic pilot Adolphe Pégoud perform at the Johannisthal aerodrome in Berlin. Fleischer was greatly inspired, and harboured hopes of becoming a flier himself. However, when the war came he served in the *Kaiser Alexander Garde Regt* Nr 1. Fleischer duly suffered through the battles of Verdun and the Somme, writing circa 1965;

'Many times, I would watch the shimmering birds high up in the air that carried on a gallant duel war with each other. I witnessed the great aces such as Boelcke, Immelmann, von Althaus and others. When I tried to transfer from my regiment to the flying corps, the answer was that I was indispensable because of the shortage of officers.'

Then in late 1916 he was wounded in the right leg by a shell splinter at the Somme. From his hospital bed he succeeded in getting his transfer to the *Fliegertruppe*. 'I was the happiest person on earth'.

After training at the *Flieger-Schule* at Zeesen and later at Gotha, he was attached to the *Flieger-Beobachter-Schule* in Königsberg during the winter of 1917-18. His personal persistence finally paid off and he went to the *Jastaschule* at Nivelles;

'Upon completion of the flying and shooting examinations, I was reassigned to *Jasta* 17. There, I was warmly greeted by Ltn Julius Buckler, who also gave me excellent and important suggestions. Now I was off on a merry pursuit! But things were altogether different than I had imagined them to be. In the beginning, my place within the *Staffel* [formation] was always in the rear, like that of a dog on a chain – you might say "the back cover". While my comrades fought often and came away with victories, I was empty-handed since I was always too late, and many times I was at the point of despair.'

By 16 April Buckler was clearly back to his best in the cockpit, claiming his 31st victory, and first since returning to the front. His opponent was a French two-seater he called a 'Breguet', which he downed at 1655 hrs near Vaux (probably Rubescourt-Vaux, to the south of Montdidier). In reality this may have been a Salmson 2A2 of *Escadrille* SAL225, as this squadron had Cpl André Ricard (pilot) and his observer Sous-Lt Paul Pruvot shot down and killed on this date.

Buckler followed this up with a Breguet five days later, on 21 April. The two-seater fell at Moreuil at 1230 hrs, giving the ace his 32nd victory. Buckler's time back at the front was to be fairly short, however, for he was soon wounded again on 3 May during an attack on a French balloon from the *67e Cié de Aerostiers* at Tricot. He recounted the event as follows;

'There was an observation balloon hanging somewhere far behind enemy lines at a considerable height. So, on 3 May I flew off at five o'clock in the morning and crossed the trenches at 2000 metres. I acted as though I did not have my eye on the balloon and kept my course somewhat to the east of it. In spite of that they did not appear to trust me over there and I noticed that the balloon was getting smaller and smaller, so they had started to haul it down. *"Malaula!"* There was no time to lose, so I swooped down upon it at full throttle.

'At about 200 metres I had it in front of me full-size. The observer had already jumped out and I was welcomed with flak and machine gun fire, but that did not disturb me. I aimed very calmly and fired 20 rounds at the balloon, then I had to pull the machine upwards otherwise so as to avoid ramming it. I had hardly passed over it when I went into a left turn, and cast a furtive glance at the envelope to see whether there were any small burning holes. It was still not on fire! I was just about to fly towards it again when I finally saw the little orange tongue of flame shoot out. I could fly home with my mind at ease.

Ltn Wilhelm Becker achieved his second, and last, victory on 1 April 1918 when he downed a French two-seater. He is pictured in the cockpit of the Albatros D V *Gisi*, with its storm cloud emblem – he may have flown this aircraft after Rudno-Rudzinski left the unit

Jasta 17 personnel soak up the spring sunshine in this view, probably taken around the beginning of May. They are, from left to right, Wilhelm Becker (standing), Ltn d R Spindler (seated), Alfred Träger (standing, hands in pockets), Alfred Fleischer, Georg Strasser, Julius Buckler, Adolf Werner, Vzfw Brendel, possibly Ltn d R Schumann (the OzbV) and *Staffelführer* Hptm Rudolf *Freiherr* von Esebeck, who would fall on 27 May 1918

'The flak was thick, and every shot signified an invitation to stick around. I had to fly in a zig-zag in order to dodge them and staggered around the sky like a drunkard. Then my left ankle was struck by a terrible blow. The pain was great but fear of getting hit a second time was greater. Greatest of all was my dread at the thought of falling into captivity. I could only steer with my right foot, as the left one was as good as dead.'

Then Buckler recounted how he had the foresight to have had a leather stirrup for each foot attached to the rudder bar – for just such an occasion as this, when one leg was crippled by a wound. It worked. 'With my right leg I was able to steer *Mops* not only over the frontlines, but all the way to the airfield'. He realised it was not a clean wound, the bullet having lodged in his left leg. This meant another long period of recovery. Buckler was taken to a field hospital, then was loaded onto a medical train and transported to a Bavarian hospital. After that he was moved to a facility at Lindau, on Lake Constance. 'The wound to my foot was more painful than all four of my earlier wounds put together', he wrote. This final injury brought Buckler the Wound Badge in Gold, signifying five or more wounds sustained during the war. He was the only 'Blue Max' airman to receive it.

At the front, meanwhile, *Jasta* 17 had once again moved, this time to Ercheu airfield on 19 May. It was still in the 18. *Armee* and was now a component of *Jagdgruppe* 11, along with *Staffeln* 48, 53 and 61. This *Jagdgruppe* was commanded by an officer familiar to the old *Jasta* 17 veterans – *Rittmeister* Heinz Anton *Freiherr* von Brederlow, the unit's very first commander from its days at Metz. Although *Freiherr* von Brederlow commanded the entire *Jagdgruppe*, he had never forgotten his old *Staffel*. In fact his brother *Rittm d R* Hans *Freiher* von Brederlow had served as *Jasta* 17's adjutant (*OzbV*) in 1917.

On 27 May the German Offensive on the Aisne (Operation *Blücher-Yorck,* or the Third Battle of the Aisne) began between Noyon and Reims. On the battle's opening day *Jasta* 17 suffered yet another devastating loss of its *Staffelführer* in combat. The highly respected and admired Rudolf *Freiherr* von Esebeck was shot down in flames during an attack on Breguet bombers near Rambercourt. The Breguet crew of Lt Charlet and Cpl Gérard of *Escadrille* BR217 claimed two fighters and one two-seater in combat, and von Esebeck was probably one of these. In a sentiment echoed by many other *Jasta* 17 veterans, Buckler wrote, 'One never heard an ill word spoken about von Esebeck. He stood up for every man in his *Staffel* whenever it mattered. What luck to have him as a superior!'

In this desperate time there was probably little opportunity for a long search for a new commander, so someone was promoted to acting leader from within the unit. Oblt Wilhelm Pritsch had only arrived at *Jasta* 17 from the *Jastaschule* on 27 April, yet he was appointed acting commander on 29 May – a post he would hold for about two weeks. As if he intended to prove he was worthy of the appointment, on 9 June Pritsch brought down a French Salmson 2A2 at 1220 hrs near Montigny. It was his first and only victory.

Pritsch relinquished his acting command of the *Staffel* on 12 June when another familiar name returned to the unit roster. Ltn d R Günther Schuster was brought back from *Jasta* 29, but now he would command his old unit. He had raised his score to five since leaving *Jasta* 17 in September 1917, downing two Camels and a SE 5a. No doubt he received a warm welcome from the old hands of all ranks.

Exactly one week earlier, on 5 June, a new pilot had arrived from AFP 5. Uffz Arnold Lilienthal would not have an outstanding career as a *Jagdflieger*, but his story deserves mention. He bore a name famous in German aviation, but was not related to the celebrated glider pioneer Otto Lilienthal. Born to a Jewish family on 23 May 1892, Lilienthal had experienced anti-Semitism from his flying instructor at Johannisthal, but he persevered and was posted to FAA 237 in early 1917. There, his competent service earned him his pilot's badge on 3 September 1917. One of his adventures in *Jasta* 17 was recounted by Felix Theilhaber in his book *Jüdische Flieger im Weltkrieg* (1924), and it is worth repeating for its information about the outdated equipment of the unit;

'One day they were flying over Noyon in two *Ketten* [flights] with no particular target in mind. Lilienthal was flying in the rear-most position in an old Albatros D V which climbed well to 3500 metres, but after that it tended to flounder.

'On this day it was very cloudy and misty, and as the aircraft raced through the air Lilienthal had looked around often without seeing an enemy behind him. Then suddenly there was a clattering and rattling noise and Lilienthal received a blow to the wrist that knocked his hand away from the controls. He quickly grabbed them with the other hand, wondering if he'd just been hit by flak. But turning around, he saw two enemy airmen who were quite comfortably firing into his crate. There was nothing to do but immediately go to into a dive, pull the machine around and climb up again. Unfortunately the Albatros couldn't climb. Lilienthal was only able to pull up, deliver a couple of shots and then tip over.

'In the meantime six sprightly creatures had assembled around the poor "hare" and shot him up properly. Lilienthal quickly considered that in a prolonged dive the wing surfaces of his Albatros would shred apart and the wings would break off. With his motor at full revs, he went down vertically on his nose after having pulled the machine over on its left wing,

Oblt Wilhelm Pritsch was appointed acting commander of the *Jasta* after *Staffelführer* von Esebeck's death on 27 May 1918. Pritsch is seen here at a later date, posing with his highly decorated Albatros-built Fokker D VII named "*Bowke!*". It displayed whimsical facial markings on the nose, inspired by the cooling holes cut into the cowling

Ltn d R Alfred Fleischer arrived at *Jasta* 17 on 12 April 1918. He is seen here with his Albatros D Va in a view dating from circa May/June 1918. His aircraft was adorned with diamonds and an 'F' emblem, both in red, as well as the usual black/white tail markings

feigning being shot down as he rushed downwards. Thus he fell, down to 1000 metres, where he began to pull the machine out. Fortunately, he was able to go down and land unmolested, but the machine cracked up during the landing as the undercarriage had been completely shot up. Forty hits by incendiary ammunition were identified.'

It appears that Lilienthal was posted out of *Jasta* 17 at some later date in the summer of 1918, and he disappears from the available records, at least until long after the war.

Since arriving at *Jasta* 17 in mid-April, Alfred Fleischer had experienced a number of unsuccessful combats, and some close calls, but as yet he had no confirmed victories. After one particularly narrow escape from enemy fighters, Buckler admonished him;

'Dear Fleischer, I had given you up for lost. Next time, keep up with the formation and pay closer attention. We are not shooting with peas!'

'Since Schuster had taken command', wrote Fleischer, 'things seemed to go much better for me as I was flying No 2 left, next to the *Staffelführer*. At last some air victories.

'We were flying seven Albatros D Vs in the direction of Soissons [on 29 June] when suddenly I observed a SPAD squadron crossing our path at about 1000 metres below. To attract the attention of my *Staffelführer*, as well as my other comrades, I tipped my wings and began shooting phosphorous ammunition, but no one responded. I then left the *Staffel* and, in a dive, singly attacked the seven SPADs. After firing my first burst, a SPAD went up almost vertically, and, with my second attack, he burst into bright flames and disappeared into the abyss. The ruckus had attracted my own squadron, and, as they approached us, the remaining SPADs took to flight.'

Fleischer's SPAD may have been the fighter of Cpl J Mandray of SPA103 (also part of the 'Storks' Group), who was killed at 1845 hrs.

Fleischer recalled that, '*Jasta* 17 was outfitted with Fokker D VIIs shortly after my first victory'. Finally, the unit had some first-class fighters. Under Günther Schuster's able command, the *Jasta* made yet another major move on 10 July. On that date it was transferred to the 3. *Armee* Front airfield at Mars sous Bourcq, south of Sedan. As the pilots of *Jasta* 17 prepared to play their parts in Ludendorff's last offensive – the so-called *Friedensturm* ('Peace Offensive') in Champagne – they knew that difficult challenges lay ahead.

FINAL DAYS

The last of Ludendorff's offensives erupted on 15 July 1918. Known as the Second Battle of the Marne, its aim was to draw Allied reserves south from Flanders and enlarge the salient created by Operation *Blücher-Yorck*. Among the German Armies involved was Karl von Einem's 3. *Armee* – it was pitted against the French 4th *Armée* (which included the American 42nd Infantry Division at this time) east of Reims. *Jasta* 17, now based at Mars sous Bourcq, would go into action against French *escadrilles* and the new US Air Service (USAS) as well.

On the day the offensive began, *Staffelführer* Günther Schuster attempted to help blind the French defenders by attacking a captive observation balloon near Suippes. Schuster was credited with destroying the 'gasbag' for his sixth, and final, victory. On that day the assault east of Reims was stopped in its tracks, but west of Reims the Germans succeeded in crossing the Marne. The advance was stalled on the 17th and a short while later Gen Ferdinand Foch launched his counter-offensive, later known as the Battle of Soissons. In the resulting retreat of German forces, *Jasta* 17 was transferred to Vivaise airfield on 25 July.

The inexperienced American airmen of the 1st Pursuit Group had moved to Touquin airfield, some 32 miles south of Chateau-Thierry, on 28 June. The Nieuport 28 pilots of the USAS's 27th Aero Squadron had been hit particularly hard in the recent fighting. The entire group was still in the process of re-equipping with SPAD XIIIs on 1 August – a date that would be remembered as the 'Black Day for the 27th Aero'. It would also involve *Jasta* 17 ace Alfred Fleischer in a fight that would have an impact on his life such as he never could have imagined.

That morning the 27th Aero Squadron sent out its 'A' and 'B' Flights to escort two Salmson 2A2s from the 1st Aero Squadron on a photographic mission to Fismes. The 27th pilots, flying a mix of Nieuport 28s and SPAD XIIIs, completed three circuits over enemy lines while the observers in the Salmson 2A2s changed film, but on the fourth circuit they were attacked by eight D VIIs from JG I east of Fère-en-Tardenois. In the carnage that followed, the 27th would lose six pilots killed or taken prisoner, five of them falling to *Jagdstaffeln* 4 and 6 of the 'Richthofen Circus'.

The last Yank pilot to fall was 1Lt Clifford A McElvain, the 'A' Flight leader. In the chaos of the fight he had eventually become separated from his companions in his Nieuport 28. Having already evaded one group of D VIIs, he later recalled 'I had had enough for one day and headed home'. That was when he encountered Fleischer and a *Kette* of *Jasta* 17 Fokkers. Both Fleischer and McElvain would survive this encounter, become friends and leave their own accounts of the engagement, which are remarkably similar;

'It is the 1st of August 1918 – cloudless sky, bright sunshine and unusual heat', wrote Fleischer. 'When the order reached

Günther Schuster's Fokker D VII (Alb), decorated with a white 'blitz' on the black fuselage, forms the backdrop for this portrait. The white radiator shell, together with a dark cowling (most likely black), was the unit marking employed on the Fokkers of *Jasta* 17. Schuster achieved his sixth victory on 15 July 1918 – the first day of the Second Battle of the Marne

Jasta 17 to head off in the direction of Soissons, where formidable air forces were reported, we climbed into our Fokkers with great joy in order to reach the cooler regions. We flew five abreast, with me in my usual place – to the left, next to our leader's aeroplane, which on this day was flown by Ltn Schuster.

'We advanced directly to the front and had almost reached an altitude of approximately 4000 metres when something very surprising occurred. Suddenly, and entirely unnoticed by all of us – probably coming directly from the sun – a small enemy biplane of unknown type [McElvain's Nieuport] dashed with lightning speed upon our leader's aeroplane and opened fire immediately at close range. An abrupt and distinctive glance backwards assured me that at that moment there was no danger for me. Therefore, eyes front and onto my hard-pressed comrade, who had already been disabled and forced to bring his smoking aeroplane down in a sudden dive.'

McElvain recalled;

'I discovered too late that I was on a collision course with a flight of five Fokker D VIIs. Coming at them out of the sun, they apparently did not see me. At that moment it seemed to me that it was too late for me to do anything but open fire, and my first burst went into the leader. I couldn't watch to see what happened to him, but I learned later from Fleischer that he was wounded and crashed, but survived.'

Staffelführer Günther Schuster had indeed been hit by McElvain's sudden attack. He brought his D VII down near Soissons to be taken to hospital. He would survive the war.

Referring to the remaining four Fokkers, McElvain stated;

'The three others simply got out of the way and circled, leaving one man [Fleischer] to deal with me himself. This was the kind of combat that you trained for and read about, but which seldom happened – a duel in the sky between two men armed with machine guns, alone and on their own, playing for keeps.'

Fleischer recalled;

'I immediately directed the fire of my two guns at our adversary, and thereby forced him away from my comrade. In order to escape my deadly barrage, my adversary climbed so steeply that he stood almost perpendicularly above me. This manoeuvre to gain safe altitude would have been achieved by him had my brave Fokker not shown an unusually marvellous performance. In great style it followed this dash for altitude and hung on its propeller so that I could cover my adversary with a well-directed and continuous fire. McElvain allowed his aeroplane to glide down over the left wing, and in this manner he escaped my fire. By this manoeuvre he reached approximately the same altitude as me, and now the advantages of my Fokker were demonstrated, which at the time – without boasting – flew to perfection.

'Persistently and with resolute determination, McElvain attempted to fight me off again and again. Closely together, we circled around each other, and often it seemed as though the world was standing on its head. The spirit of the chase gripped me. However, because of the excellent manoeuvring and, above all, my adversary's persistence to fight on,

Jagdstaffel 17 commander Ltn d R Günther Schuster was wounded by McElvain's attack in the combat of 1 August. He may have been flying his black Albatros-built D VII with the lightning bolt emblem, as seen in this fine view. Schuster brought his aircraft down safely near Soissons. He survived the war but died at Castelnova di Sotto, in Italy, on 8 October 1943

I succeeded in firing a few poorly aimed shots. I believe McElvain had similar experiences. How long this circular battle continued, I do not know.'

McElvain told a similar story;

'I was very light in both fuel and ammunition by now, so my Nieuport was especially agile. Fleischer's Fokker D VII was faster and could out-climb me. It was only this summer that I learned from Fleischer that his Fokker was supercharged [it was fitted with a 185 hp BMW IIIa engine]. We met at about 13,000 ft, and at that altitude his supercharger gave him a considerable advantage in climb and speed, but even so our aeroplanes were pretty well matched – he could out-climb and out-dive me, I could make tighter turns. It was a fair match, I think.

'It seemed that the fight would never end because our aeroplanes were so evenly matched that it was very hard for either of us to get a chance at a shot. Fleischer said that I got a few holes in his aeroplane, and he scattered some splinters over me when one of his bullets hit a wooden longeron in my fuselage, but no real damage was done to either machine.'

Then Fleischer got lucky;

'At an altitude of approximately 300 to 450 metres, I was successful, after having completed a reverse ascending curve, to place several well-directed shots. Soon thereafter McElvain exposed himself in a manner at first entirely incomprehensible to me [the Nieuport had in fact run out of fuel]. I was able to gain a position 35 to 45 metres behind him, and had already aimed my machine guns upon him, ready to pull the triggers in the fever of the chase. There, I beheld, thank God, in the last moment that the propeller of my adversary stood still and that the aeroplane, completely out of control, prepared to land.'

McElvain explained;

'Then without any warning my engine suddenly blooped and died, and there I was in combat without power and losing altitude fast. The Nieuport was fitted with a low-compression engine, so my propeller continued to windmill and my guns would still fire – Fleischer had no way to know the fight was over, and he chased me right to the ground. Finally, when the time came that I had to straighten out for a crash-landing, Fleischer moved behind me and I sat there waiting for the crash ahead, and at the same time expecting the bullets from behind that would keep me from feeling it. It was only when I slowed down for the crash that my propeller slowed and stopped, and at that last instant the Fokker dived past me and the pilot waved. He had seen my propeller stop and he knew I was through.'

Fleischer said that as soon as he had seen McElvain's propeller stop;

'For me, as for every other German soldier, there was no only one thing to do – to stop the battle immediately and to shake the hand of the defeated adversary in a chivalrous manner. A few minutes later the Nieuport crashed into a small wooded area. Uninjured, McElvain climbed out of the wreckage and waved to me above, probably with mixed feelings.

1Lt Clifford A McElvain, 'A' Flight Leader of the 27th Aero Squadron, is pictured with his mechanics and an unidentified Nieuport 28. He would encounter Alfred Fleischer on the 'Black Day' for the 27th Aero Squadron, 1 August 1918

Alfred Fleischer of *Jasta* 17 would fight an epic duel with Clifford McElvain of the 27th Aero Squadron on 1 August. Fleischer's Albatros-built Fokker D VII displayed the black and white nose of the *Staffel*, as well as a triangular emblem and fuselage trim that is believed to have been yellow in colour

1Lt Clifford McElvain is seen with his Nieuport 28 N6214, squadron number '5'. This is the machine he was flying on 1 August 1918 when he fought his duel with Alfred Fleischer (*A Toelle*)

'I was far behind the German front in the vicinity of some pieces of heavy artillery. Soon I found a suitable place where I could land. When I looked over my bird, I was happy to find that there were only a few holes in the wings. Then I went over to McElvain, who – rather fatigued, though smiling – stepped towards me. Impulsively and cordially, like two good old friends, we shook hands and smiled like two boys after a successfully completed adventure.

'After we had carried on our conversation for quite some time with the help of an interpreter and exchanged our addresses, we parted with the feeling that a friendship had been founded that would become inseparable. I should have liked to take McElvain with me as my guest to my squadron. This, however, to my regret was impossible. Once more I waved goodbye to McElvain while circling around the spot, and then returned to our flying field.'

McElvain went off to a PoW camp, being released in November 1918. He would see Fleischer again, however.

According to Fleischer, Schuster had 'escaped serious injury', but he was hospitalised. The command of *Jasta* 17 passed, at long last, to the recently returned Ltn d R Julius Buckler – at least, that is what he says in *'Malaula!'* As the unit's highest scorer by far, and a reserve officer with the *Pour le Mérite,* he certainly seems to have been the most qualified. However, at least one between-the-wars German *Jasta* researcher suggested that Schuster returned and Buckler was never actually in official, full command of the *Staffel.* On the other hand he is listed as the final *Staffelführer* in both Wasenmüller's history and Zuerl's *Pour le Mérite Flieger*, and he was referred to as the *Jasta* commander by Fleischer and other contemporaries. This author believes that Buckler did indeed command the unit in the last three months of the war, and he certainly led it in the air.

Besides Fleischer and Bohny, Buckler had one other standout flier in his ranks, and he was a recent arrival. Vzfw Hans Christian Friedrich Donhauser was born on 9 September 1894. Apparently he was the Gefr (later Uffz) Donhauser who flew with AA 221 in early 1917. If so, then he distinguished himself on a reconnaissance mission made on 6 April 1917, with Ltn Wilhelm Wolter as his observer. During a hot combat with an enemy fighter, Donhauser's two-seater took more than 40 hits, the flare storage box was set on fire and Wolter was wounded in the right arm and chest. Donhauser still managed to land the smoking machine and brought Wolter to medical help, saving his life.

Donhauser was apparently slightly wounded himself on 5 June 1917, after which he was sent off to a flying school – perhaps as an instructor. He seems to have returned to the front as a pilot with FA 10 by May 1918, when he and observer Ltn Hempler shot down a SPAD (although this is generally not listed among his official victories). This helped earn Donhauser a posting to *Jastaschule* 1, and from there he came to *Jasta* 17 circa late June/early July 1918. Ambitious and cocky, he would not waste much time in making a name for himself.

Fleischer achieved his third confirmed victory during the evening of 19 August. Many years later he would recall, 'In the middle of August 1918, on a late afternoon, a great air battle took place in the area south of Château Thierry. There were approximately 60 to 70 aeroplanes of all types'. Fleischer shot down a SPAD XIII at Château Thierry, apparently flown by MdL Maurice Caulier of *Escadrille* SPA94, who was captured.

On 20 August Vzfw Christian Donhauser began his meteoric climb to fame when he received his first confirmation for a French Breguet downed behind French lines at 1855 hrs. Donhauser was both very aggressive and very lucky in attaining confirmations in the hectic and often confused final months of the war. Two days after *Luftsieg* number one, Donhauser knocked down a SPAD at 1135 hrs over Soissons – after that, there was no stopping him. On 25 August he chalked up his first 'double' when he was credited with a 'Breguet' at Audignicourt at 1145 hrs. This was much more likely a Salmson 2A2 from *Escadrille* SAL18, as that unit lost the crew of Brig Pierre Fournillon (pilot) and Aspirant Victor Bogry, both of whom were killed. Donhauser's second victory later that day was a SPAD fighter over Vézaponin at 1835 hrs. The next day he repeated his feat with a balloon at Carlepont at 2000 hrs, followed by a SPAD that was attempting to defend the 'gasbag' southwest of Cuts only five minutes later.

On the 27th Donhauser destroyed another SPAD (northwest of Terny at 1910 hrs) that is tentatively identified as the aircraft of Adj L Hannebicque of SPA93, who went missing in action. Two days later Donhauser claimed another SPAD over St Paul aux Bois (not credited in some sources). On 30 August Karl Bohny took a bit of the limelight from Donhauser when he bagged a SPAD of his own at Bagneux at 1855 hrs for his fourth credited opponent. Not to be outdone, Donhauser successfully claimed a Breguet about 75 minutes later over Cuts.

2 September was a very active day for the pilots of *Jasta* 17, and for once Donhauser was unlucky. Two new pilots chalked up their first and only successes. In the morning Gefr Jacob downed a SPAD fighter at Savigny at 1100 hrs. In the evening Donhauser and Flgr Fritz Wolff (no relation

Julius Buckler returned to the *Jasta* on 5 August 1918. Most accounts record that he commanded the *Staffel* for the final three months of the war, although some historians have disputed this

A mix of Albatros and OAW-built D VIIs is seen on the airfield at Vivaise, occupied by *Jasta* 17 from 25 July to 25 September. Pritsch's Fokker is fifth from right, and Schuster's black machine with the lightning bolt is at the extreme left

Vzfw Hans Christian Friedrich Donhauser went on an impressive scoring spree in August and September 1918. This Sanke postcard view (Number 677) was one of the last of its type issued during the war. The Fokker D VII in the background displays the white radiator shell and black nose of *Staffel* 17. Historian Lance Bronnenkant has determined that the '17' on Donhauser's arm patch was actually retouched in over a '10' dating from his previous service in FA 10

Equipped with the superb Fokker D VII, the pilots of *Jasta* 17 were still a force to be reckoned with in the war's final months. Oblt Wilhelm Pritsch strikes a confident pose aboard his D VII (Alb) named *"Bowke!"*. It also displayed a swastika and the usual *Staffel* unit colours on the nose. The significance of the *"Bowke!"* legend remains unknown. It was likely a nonsense word of arcane meaning, like 'Malaula!'

to the 'elderly' Wolff of earlier days) were in combat. Wolff shot down a SPAD at 1930 hrs at Savigny. At precisely the same time Donhauser claimed another SPAD, followed by a Breguet 30 minutes later, but both of those claims were denied.

The commander of *Jagdgruppe* 11 was *Rittm* Heinz Anton von Brederlow, who had commanded *Jasta* 17 at the time of its formation. Now, on 3 September, he successfully downed a SPAD XIII at Soissons for what is believed to be his one and only victory. That same day the consistently deadly Donhauser destroyed another SPAD – very likely the aircraft of Cpl Roger Pradel of SPA96, who was listed as missing in action. Donhauser claimed yet another SPAD the following day, but failed to have it confirmed.

On 25 September *Jasta* 17 was ordered to move yet again as Germany's fortunes waned. The *Staffel* relocated to Chuffilly in the 3. *Armee* sector, and the squadron lost Uffz Janzen who was injured in a crash. Eight days later, 'Little' Karl Bohny achieved ace status when he forced a SPAD down in the morning for his fifth. The next day – 4 October – the pilots of *Jasta* 17 mauled a flight of SPADs from *Escadrille* SPA93. Alfred Fleischer got his fourth victory, Karl Bohny his sixth and Ltn d R Karl Kaiser his first (and only) kill. These three claims can be matched to at least two known losses suffered by SPA93, namely Cpl Alphonse Lambert and Adj Pierre Delage, who were both listed as missing in action. Perhaps this was the episode Fleischer recalled many years later (with a little exaggeration) when he wrote;

'We shot down a complete *Spadstaffel* with the exception of the commanding officer. We were in combat with six SPADs, one of which I forced down behind the front. The pilot, a French corporal, was slightly wounded, although his aeroplane was completely demolished. I landed beside the crashed fighter, but all the pilot would say was *"Malheur la guerre!"* And though I tried, I was unable to get his name.'

The *Staffel* was really hitting its stride, for on 5 October the unit notched up another three victories for a total of six in two days. Buckler was back in his old form, despatching a Salmson 2A2 from SAL27 at 1715 hrs for his 34th confirmed victory. At almost the same time Karl Bohny shot down another Salmson from the same unit (although both victims were misidentified as 'AR' machines). SAL27 lost two crews killed in action. Four hours before this encounter, Donhauser had downed a SPAD, and he would follow it up with a Breguet on the evening of 7 October. On the 9th he was awarded the prestigious Golden Military Merit Cross.

Two days later, the *Staffel* was forced to shift aerodromes yet again, as Germany's forces retreated. *Jasta* 17 remained in the 3. *Armee* but transferred to the airfield at Malmy-Chémery. Nonetheless the *Jasta* 17 pilots kept up their defiant struggle. Vzfw Donhauser had something of a field day on 18 October, being credited with both a SPAD fighter and a 'SPAD two-seater' at around 1530 hrs, followed by a Breguet less than three hours later. On the 23rd Donhauser obtained credit for a SPAD at Vrizy. This was his final confirmed claim, the sketchy *Jasta* 17 war diary giving him a total of 19 victories, but only 15 or 16 were officially confirmed.

On 24 October *Staffelführer* Buckler neared the end of his amazing career as a *Jagdflieger* by downing a Breguet near Méry for his 34th or 35th confirmed claim. This machine may have come from BR257, and the victory put him in the top tier of surviving German aces. On the 30th of the month Karl Bohny flamed a French balloon at 1730 hrs at Avancon for his eighth, and last, victory. Some sources give Buckler credit for a victory on this date, and he himself wrote, 'On 30 October 1918 I shot down my 42nd opponent, and therewith attained my 35th confirmed victory'.

Jasta 17 operated a few examples of the Pfalz D XII in the war's final months. D XII 1416/18 was identified by a personal white fuselage band, as well at the unit's usual nose markings

Fleischer's fifth and sixth victories, the final confirmed ones for *Jasta* 17, came on 3 November as conditions both at the front and in Germany itself were degenerating into chaos. He was given credit for a brace of two-seaters. Fleischer may have been recalling one of these in later years when he wrote;

'We had seven Fokkers in the air and were under orders to attack the numerous enemy reconnoitering aeroplanes. These were usually strongly fortified with flight protection. One had to be careful as hell to avoid being shot down. Without being observed, I managed to leave the formation and go down on a DH 4 that had been left unprotected. Coming from above and to the rear, I positioned myself directly underneath its body and effectively shot from a very close distance (about 50 metres), whereupon, the aeroplane reared straight up and turned slowly over on its back. With that, the observer fell out and dropped like a rock past me into the crater [area of the front]. Following him was the heavily-shot up aeroplane in a steep spiral, with a fully running motor, that soon smashed into small fragments in the combat area.'

On 8 November Buckler wrote;

'I led the united *Staffel* once more to the front. While doing so I shot down my 43rd opponent. It was no longer possible to obtain confirmation, and after landing I found a telephone message waiting for me that I should report immediately to the *Kommandeur der Flieger.*'

Buckler managed to reach the *Kofl* at Charleroi after forcing his way past mobs of revolutionary-minded infantry. He was informed of the chaos in Germany and the mutinies in the German Navy, and was told to go back and await developments.

Exactly two years after *Jasta* 17 had been declared operational it was all over on 11 November 1918. Buckler wrote that previously, plans had been made to celebrate the anniversary, 'but there was no mood for celebration on this day. The festivities rather resembled a funeral'. *Jagdstaffel* 17 was credited with 101 confirmed victories (87 aircraft and 14 balloons), three aircraft 'forced to land' (*zLgzw*) and a further 18 victories that could not be confirmed.

Things are not always as they seem. This could easily be a wartime view of Christian Donhauser with a BMW-engined Fokker D VII. However, it actually dates from December 1918, when Donhauser was test-flying aircraft that were being turned over to American forces at Coblenz. He was *Jasta* 17's star during the war's final months, quickly chalking up at least 15 confirmed victories in only 60 days

Christian Donhauser became a celebrity of sorts among the Americans he met in Coblenz in December 1918 (where he was testing aircraft that were being delivered to US forces) by claiming to have downed Quentin Roosevelt, the son of the 26th president. Here, Donhauser poses with Yank observer ace Lt Arthur Easterbrook of the 1st Aero Squadron. American journalist Damon Runyon interviewed Donhauser in Coblenz, reporting that, 'he is a little fellow, about as cocky as they come' (*A Toelle*)

EPILOGUE

The post-war lives of some of the prominent *Jasta* 17 pilots took widely differing paths. After a brief time in the automotive industry, Julius Buckler became a flying instructor with the *Deutsche Verkehrsfliegerschule* at Staaken. In 1924 he worked briefly as a pilot in the Soviet Union with his old friend Strasser. By 1928 Buckler was a director of a Berlin road construction firm, which led to profitable work in the asphalt industry building airport runways.

In the early 1930s he joined the *SA-Fliegersturm,* which later became a flying formation of the SS. In 1933 Buckler received his new pilot's license, and in 1934 he became a captain in the *Deutscher Luftsportverband* (German Aerial Sport Association). By 1937 he was entertaining German crowds at flying displays as a *Nationalsozialistisches Fliegerkorps* unit leader. Buckler was commissioned as a major in the Luftwaffe, and during World War 2 he was a special duties officer at the *Jagdfliegerschule* in Werneuchen, then an instructor in the commander's office in Staaken. He became a Headquarters Commander, Airfield Command 42/III in early 1944.

After the war Buckler returned to the asphalt and road construction industry, but he renewed his pilot's license in 1955 and continued to engage in sport flying until 1960. He had married Erica, Baronness von Braun and the marriage produced a son, Michael. Buckler died at Bad Godesberg on 23 May 1960.

His close friend Georg Strasser struggled in the difficult economic times that followed the war. He briefly flew as an airmail pilot for the *Luft-Reederei* in 1919, and occasionally found work as an exhibition pilot in Germany and the Netherlands, once saving his life by parachute. Strasser married Gertrud Parge, the widow of a Fokker test pilot killed in an accident, and started a family. In 1922 he found work as a test and delivery pilot with the Junkers firm in Dessau. However, on 4 December 1925 he crashed on takeoff in a Junkers F 13 and died shortly thereafter at the age of 34.

Christian Donhauser added a curious postscript to his career immediately after the war. Commissioned as a leutnant in the postwar *Reichswehr*, he was one of the pilots detailed to test fly aircraft that were being handed over to the Americans. Trainloads of Fokker D VIIs and other machines were delivered to Coblenz in accord with the terms of the Armistice, and were assembled at nearby Fort Kaiser Alexander to be test-flown by German pilots before acceptance. In December 1918 Donhauser was one such pilot, and thus became acquainted with many US airmen at Coblenz. He boasted that he was the victor over 30 aircraft, and brashly bragged that one of his victims was Quentin Roosevelt.

Quentin Roosevelt of the USAS's 27th Aero Squadron had been shot down and killed on 14 July 1918. He was, of course, the fourth son of former president Theodore Roosevelt. Being one of the most popular and charismatic figures in the USAS, his death was a national tragedy. Roosevelt had, in fact, been brought down by Vzfw Emil Gräper of *Jasta* 50, and Donhauser's first confirmed victory had not been attained until 20 August. Donhauser's false claim to have killed Roosevelt, and his cocky attitude, earned him instant notoriety (much of it negative) among the US airmen at Coblenz, and he became the subject of several American newspaper articles and official photos. Donhauser was injured at Coblenz on 1 January 1919 in the crash of Roland D VIb 6141/18 – he broke a wrist and several ribs. Donhauser continued to fly after his recovery, only to be killed in a crash at Schleissheim on 14 August 1919. He is buried in the *Neuer Friedhof* in Hamburg-Harburg.

Jewish pilot Jakob Wolff was 49 years old by war's end. He had been discharged following his recuperation, having been awarded the Iron Cross 1st and 2nd Class, the Hamburg *Hanseatenkreuz*, the Turkish *Rote Halbmond* and the Knight 2nd Class with Swords of the White Falcon Order of the Grand Duchy of Saxe-Weimar-Einsach. He returned to run his successful cigar factory in Hamburg, and in the economically difficult times of the early 1920s he gave employment to his old *Kampfstaffel* Metz comrade Bruno Loerzer. Wolff and his wife Elsa had a son, Eberhart, and Wolff actively promoted German aviation during its low ebb – his firm had several factory aircraft. He died on 4 December 1926.

Wolff's wife subsequently remarried, and through the intervention of Bruno Loerzer and Hermann Göring, her son and his two sisters were officially declared 'of German Blood' by edict of the *Führer*. Eberhart joined the Luftwaffe in 1940 and died as a member of *Kampfstaffel* 1/106 in May 1942.

The other Jewish *Jagdflieger* of *Jasta* 17, Arnold Lilienthal, met a tragic end. At age 51 he was transported from Berlin to the ghetto in Lodz, Poland, in December 1941. He died in Lodz on 28 April 1942, a victim of the Holocaust.

The remarkable tale of Alfred Fleischer will bring this volume to an end. In 1933 Fleischer was a Luftwaffe major and chief of air police at Berlin's Tempelhof Airport. His American victim, Lt Clifford McElvain (then commanding an Air National Guard squadron in Chicago), managed to make contact with him, and the two renewed their friendship through a series of letters. During World War 2 both men served again in their respective air forces, both rising to the rank of colonel.

In 1945 Fleischer was in an Austrian village when he surrendered to American forces. He could not return to his Silesian home – now in Soviet territory – and his wife was a prisoner of the Russians, while their son Günther was also an American PoW. Miraculously, in 1946-47 he was reunited with his family, but now faced a crisis with no job and no future in post-war Germany. He wrote to McElvain in Chicago, who immediately sent food and aid through friends. McElvain also arranged for the Fleischers to be employed by the US military government. Finally, at McElvain's suggestion, Alfred Fleischer and his family came to Chicago in 1950. Günther Fleischer became an American citizen employed by McElvain's mortgage company.

Alfred Fleischer returned to Germany with his wife in 1961, but he would return to Chicago occasionally and relive his adventures with his old friend McElvain at meetings of the Chicago Cross & Cockade Society. He died in Germany on 11 June 1978.

Old adversaries, and comrades, Clifford McElvain (left) and Alfred Fleischer revive old memories at a meeting of the Midwest Chapter of the Cross & Cockade Society in Chicago, circa 1961. McElvain was instrumental in bringing Fleischer's family to the US in the troubled times after World War 2, and the two remained lifelong friends (*R Sheldon*)

APPENDICES

Aces who served in *Kampfstaffel* Metz*

Name	Eventual Victories	Notes
Ltn Joachim von Bertrab	5	Victories achieved in *Jasta* 30
Ltn Hermann Göring	22	*Jastas* 5, 26, 27, JG I CO, PLM
Vzfw Hans Imelmann	6	*Jasta* 2
Oblt Stefan Kirmaier	11	*KEK* Jametz, *Jasta* 6, *Jasta* 2 CO
Oblt Bruno Loerzer	44	*Jasta* 5, Js 26, JG III CO, PLM
Gefr Fritz Loerzer	11	*Jasta 6*, CO of *Jastas* 63 and 26

* None of these men attained any confirmed victories while in *Kampfstaffel* Metz, but they later achieved prominence in other units.
Göring and Bruno Loerzer are sometimes listed as members of *Jasta* 17, but this most likely resulted from confusion with *Kampfstaffel* Metz

Aces who served in *Jagdstaffel* 17*

Names	Victories in *Jasta* 17	Overall Victories
Ltn Karl Bohny	6	8
Ltn d R Julius Buckler	35/36	35/36
Vzfw Christian Donhauser	16/19	16/19
Ltn d R Otto Fitzner	3	9
Ltn d R Alfred Fleischer	6	6
Vzfw Fritz John Jacobsen	0	8
Vzfw Gustav Schniedewind	4	7
Ltn d R Herbert Schröder	0	5
Ltn d R Günther Schuster	3	6
Vzfw Georg Strasser	7	7

* Listed in alphabetical order. As always, there is some controversy and disagreement about the true victory scores of some of these men. Buckler himself stated he had 35, while some sources give him 36. Donhauser's score is variously given as anything from 15 or 16 to 19, while he himself claimed 30 in post-war interviews!

Notes on *Jasta* 17 Aircraft

Aircraft	Pilot(s)	Details
Halberstadt D II 115/16	Strasser	flown 17/11/16
Albatros D II 502/16	Strasser	flown 11/3/17
Albatros D II 518/16	Jacobsen, Strasser	flown by Strasser 4/3/17
Albatros D II 520/16	Strasser	4/3/17
Albatros D II (OAW) 933/16	J Wolff	crashed 8/2/17
Albatros D II (OAW) 935/16	Strasser	flown 2/17
Albatros D II 1700/16	Strasser	flown 29/1/17
Albatros D II 1705/16	unknown	–
Albatros D II 1710/16	unknown	–
Albatros D II 1712/16	Strasser	flown 11/16 to 2/17, 1 victory
Albatros D II 1722/16	Strasser	flown 28/3/17
Albatros D II 1725/16	Strasser	flown 2/17
Albatros D II 1727/16	Gros, Strasser	flown by Strasser 3-4/17
Albatros D III 2027/16	unknown	–

Albatros D III 2032/16	Strasser	flown 19/2/17 to 23/3/17, 1 victory
Albatros D III 2033/16	Buckler	*Mops*, also flown by Strasser on 3/6/17
Albatros D III 2133/16	unknown	damaged, later in *Jasta* 37 in 9/17
Albatros D III 2177/16	Strasser	flown in 5-6/17
Albatros D III 2289/16	Strasser	flown 5/17, shot up 23/5/27
Albatros D III 2291/16	Strasser	flown 25-27/5/17
Albatros D III 2301/16	Strasser	flown from AFP 7 on 14/4/17
Albatros D V 2010/17	Strasser	collected from AFP 4 on 5/7/17
Albatros D V 2025/17	Strasser	flown 9/7 to 27/8/17, 2 victories
Albatros D V 4408/17	Strasser	flown 22/8/17 to 2/2/18, 2 victories
Albatros D V 4646/17	Strasser	delivered from AFP 4 on 11/10/17
Pfalz D III 1428/17	Fitzner	crashed at Wasquehal 30/9/17
Pfalz D IIIa 4218/17	unknown	transferred from *Jasta* 24 on 29/1/18
Pfalz D IIIa 4287, 4289 and 4294/17	unknown	transferred from *Jasta* 24 on 29/1/18
Pfalz D XII 1416/18	unknown	–
Pfalz D XII 2623/18	unknown	recorded on strength on 13/11/18 18
Fokker D VII (OAW) 4166/18	unknown	photographed late 1918

The following Fokker D VIIs were recorded as on strength on 13 November 1918 as the *Staffel* prepared to demobilise and return home. Pilots are unknown;

Fokker D VII (Alb) 5202/18
Fokker D VII (Alb) 5211/18
Fokker D VII (Alb) 5216/18
Fokker D VII (Alb) 5438/18
Fokker D VII (Alb) 5454/18
Fokker D VII (OAW) 6329/18

Fokker D VII (OAW) 6357/18
Fokker D VII (OAW) 6587/18
Fokker D VII (OAW) 6591/18
Fokker D VII (OAW) 6592/18
Fokker D VII (OAW) 6596/18

COLOUR PLATES

All of the art in this section was meticulously created by Harry Dempsey, who patiently collaborated with the writer to illustrate the aircraft and markings as accurately as currently possible. The colours depicted are often approximations based on the available data and interpretation of photographs. Many details are, as a result, provisional. The author owes a great debt to the research of such authorities as Manfred Thiemeyer, Bruno Schmäling, Reinhard Zankl, Ray Rimell, Josef Scott, Colin Owers and the late Alex Imrie and Dan-San Abbott. Any errors are entirely the author's responsibility.

1
Fokker E III (serial unknown) of Vzfw Jakob Wolff, *Kampfstaffel* Metz, Metz-Frescaty, *circa* August 1916
The serial number of this rather worn Fokker is a mystery, but it most likely came from the E III batch numbered 601-636/15. As is typical of this early period, the aircraft displayed no distinctive markings, save for the extensive castor oil staining on the fuselage! The true nature of the beige colour of the fabric is currently a matter of debate among enthusiasts. These monoplanes may have simply been covered with clear-doped unbleached linen fabric, but the opaque nature of the covering suggests that the linen was either dyed or colour doped after being attached to the airframe, then clear-doped and varnished. Wolff may have been flying this E III when he claimed his first unconfirmed victory on 16 August.

2
Albatros D II 1712/16 of Vzfw Georg Strasser, *Jasta* 17, Metz-Frescaty, December 1916
Strasser flew this machine extensively from late November 1916 to mid-February 1917, and scored his first *Luftsieg* with it. Like most D IIs of the unit, it had a clear-varnished plywood-covered fuselage and the standard Albatros reddish-brown and dark and light green camouflage on the upper wing surfaces. The rudder was probably painted in the camouflage colour of reddish-brown/Venetian red. The broad white band with two narrow black(?) bands is seen on several other D IIs, and is presumed to have been a form of *Kette* marking utilised by the *Staffel*. A black number '3' was painted on the fuselage as an individual identification marking. The struts and all metal panels were factory-finished in typical flat greenish-grey.

3
Albatros D II 1727/16 of Ltn d R Wilhelm Gros, *Jasta* 17, Metz-Frescaty, *circa* December 1916
Although this aircraft was a close 'sister' to Strasser's 1712/16, it did not have the side-mounted Windhoff radiators but rather the newer wing-mounted radiator. When photographed it displayed an immaculate varnished fuselage, with a number '1' marking and the two-colour fuselage bands seen before. In other aspects it was very similar to Strasser's D II. Gros was an experienced and capable *Kette* leader within the *Jasta*. This

91

machine was later re-marked with a '2' instead of a '1', and had the cross style updated. Georg Strasser also flew this machine five times in February-March 1917.

4

Albatros D II 1722/16 of Vzfw Georg Strasser, *Jasta* 17, St Quentin-le-Petit, March 1917

Readers are advised that Strasser's association with this aircraft is tenuous at best, for it shows up in his logbook only once, on 28 March 1917. This machine displayed a different format of fuselage band marking (also seen on several other D IIs) of a black(?) zigzag superimposed on the white band instead of stripes. Ahead of the cross was a black '2'. It had the usual finish otherwise, with dark-coloured wheel covers.

5

Albatros D II 520/16, pilot unknown, *Jasta* 17, Metz-Frescaty, February 1917

Although its usual pilot has not been identified, this Albatros has been selected to portray yet another variation on the coloured vertical bands seen on so many *Jasta* 17 machines from this period. Photographs reveal that initially 520/16 had the familiar white band with two dark stripes. However, at some later date it was re-painted with a black and white band in the proportions of the Iron Cross Medal ribbon as exhibited here. The rudder was a light colour, perhaps the pale green used in the camouflage finish, with the Albatros logo in the corner. The wheel covers were probably the undersurface pale blue.

6

Albatros D II (OAW) 933/16 of Vzfw Jakob Wolff, *Jasta* 17, Metz-Frescaty, February 1917

This aircraft was manufactured by the OAW subsidiary in Schneidemühl, and displayed the camouflage and national markings peculiar to D IIs from that factory. All the national insignia on this D II (including those under the bottom wing) were marked with narrow white borders. The fuselage cross was farther forward than on Johannisthal products, permitting the usual identification band to be painted aft of the fuselage cross – it was a black(?) band with a thin white stripe running through the middle of it. An individual '2' was painted on the fuselage just aft of the cockpit. This D II had a centrally mounted upper wing radiator, and the wing and tailplane/elevators were painted in the characteristic OAW patterns. The latter consisted of (according to a British report on an OAW-built Albatros C III) 'large patches of burnt sienna and light and dark green blending into one another. Undersides very pale blue'.

7

Albatros D II 518/16 of Vzfw Fritz John Jacobsen and Vzfw Rieger, *Jasta* 17, Metz-Frescaty, *circa* December 1916

Vzfw Rieger was photographed in what is thought to have been this D II at Metz-Frescaty airfield, and it was (apparently) later flown by Jacobsen too. The fighter was also flown at least once in March 1917 by Strasser. Its fuselage was marked with the white band with a dark zigzag and a black '1'. The wheel covers were probably pale blue, while the rudder was dark reddish-brown, with no evidence of an Albatros logo. It is believed that Jacobsen took 518/16 with him when he left *Jasta* 17 and eventually brought it to *Jasta* 31.

8

Albatros D III 2033/16 of Vzfw Julius Buckler, *Jasta* 17, St Quentin-le-Petit, April 1917

Buckler wrote that his D II fighters were named *Mops*, but unfortunately no photographs of any such D IIs have emerged. However, his D III 2033/16 is well documented. The name *Mops* was applied to the fuselage in black, ahead of the familiar broad white band with two dark vertical stripes. The rudder was covered in clear-doped fabric and the top surfaces of the wings and tailplane were camouflaged in the standard three-tone pattern of dark olive green, light Brunswick green and Venetian red/chestnut brown, with light blue undersides. The particular camouflage pattern depicted in the top view of this aeroplane is somewhat speculative. At some point in this machine's career, a bullet hole patch in the form of a small cockade was painted on the starboard side of the vertical fin, just touching the leading edge of the cross insignia.

9

Albatros D III (serial unknown) of *Rittm* Heinz Anton von Brederlow, *Jasta* 17, St Quentin-le-Petit, *circa* March 1917

Staffelführer von Brederlow was photographed with this machine, but the shot leaves much to our imagination. The only visible marking was a fuselage band in the proportions of the Iron Cross medal ribbon – a very common emblem. The tail of this D III is not visible in the photograph, so much of this profile is provisional. The wings and probably the tailplane would have borne the standard three-tone camouflage on the uppersurfaces, with light blue undersides.

10

Albatros D III (serial unknown) of Ltn d R Günther Schuster, *Jasta* 17, St-Quentin-le-Petit, June 1917

Like Buckler, many *Jasta* 17 pilots chose to christen their aircraft with a personal name that was painted on the fuselage. Schuster was photographed in an immaculate white-painted D III appropriately named *Virginal*. Strasser's logbook recorded that he also flew this aircraft at least once, but it was probably primarily flown by Schuster. The latter was, reportedly, a skilled musician, and *Virginal* is said to have been a reference to a small, antique harpsichord that he played. We have chosen to depict the vertical tail surfaces as painted in the same white as the fuselage, but this remains speculative. This D III may have survived into the period when the tails were painted black as a unit marking. The wings retained their factory-applied three-tone camouflage finish, and this may have been true of the horizontal tail surfaces as well.

11

Albatros D III (OAW) 1694/17 of Ltn Alfred Träger, *Jasta* 17, St Quentin-le Petit(?), *circa* June 1917

At some point in mid-to-late 1917, the *Staffel* adopted a unit marking of a black tail unit. The black colour was applied to the vertical tail surfaces and adjacent fuselage, and sometimes to the tailplane and elevators as well. Träger's D III was an OAW-built version which had the rounded rudder generally associated with the D V types. The forward position of the fuselage cross was also characteristic of OAW-built D IIIs. The identification emblem was, once again, a black and white fuselage band in the format of an Iron Cross ribbon. The wings were probably covered in a two-tone olive green and mauve camouflage, with the wavy demarcation lines typical of OAW-built machines.

12

Albatros D V (serial unknown) of Hptm d R Eberhard von Seel, Jasta 17, St Quentin-le-Petit, June 1917

During his brief stint as commander of the Staffel, von Seel was photographed with this beautifully decorated early production D V. The fuselage was painted in vertical stripes, which are assumed to have been black and white. The spinner, all struts and wheel covers were apparently black as well, along with the tail assembly. The wings remained in standard green and mauve camouflage on top with light blue undersides.

13

Albatros D V (serial unknown) of Ltn d R Wilhelm Gros, Jasta 17, Ghistelles, circa August 1917

This D V had longitudinal stripes (which we have interpreted as black) lengthwise over its clear-varnished fuselage, with a black tail. Like von Seel's Albatros, this was an early D V with a headrest behind the cockpit. Wheel covers were probably black as well. The wings would have retained their standard factory-applied green/mauve camouflage pattern.

14

Albatros D V (serial unconfirmed) of Vzfw Georg Strasser, Jasta 17, Wasquehal, late August 1917

Strasser was photographed with this machine at Wasquehal airfield, which the Staffel occupied in late August 1917. He had been flying D V 2025/17 since 5 July, and he flew the fighter to Wasquehal on 27 August, but that was the last flight he recorded in it. This photograph may indeed show 2025/17 as some say. However, Strasser had picked up a new D V, 4408/17, from the Flug Park on 22 August, and he also flew that machine to Wasquehal on the same day as 2025/17. He flew 4408/17 fairly exclusively from September 1917 through to January 1918, so it seems possible this aircraft is indeed 4408/17 in an early guise. The D V displayed the usual black stripe of the unit, and it also bore a dark stripe just ahead of the fuselage cross and a dark spinner that we have provisionally chosen to depict as red, but this is not confirmed. The wings were the usual green/mauve camouflage on top and pale blue beneath.

15

Albatros D V (serial unknown) of Offz Stv Julius Buckler, Jasta 17, Wasquehal, circa August 1917

Another Mops flown by Buckler was also photographed at Wasquehal, this particular aeroplane being decorated with the Staffel insignia of a black tail as well as the pilot's legend in white on a two-colour fuselage band. The colours of this band are unrecorded, and we have somewhat arbitrarily chosen to portray the band as red and blue. The wings are believed to have been finished in green/mauve camouflage with light blue undersides.

16

Albatros D V (serial unknown), pilot unknown, Jasta 17, Wasquehal, October 1917

This unidentified D V displayed the squadron's black tail, as well as a black spinner. The stripes running along the fuselage were white with (presumably) black borders. The non-striped portions of the fuselage retained the yellowish varnished plywood finish. The wings of this flamboyantly decorated machine are provisionally portrayed as green/mauve and light blue.

17

Albatros D V (serial unknown) of Ltn Alfred Träger, Jasta 17, Wasquehal, circa September 1917

Träger chose to identify his D V with the name 'Sonnenvogel' (sunbird) and decorate its fuselage with a bright sunburst emblem. This is tentatively depicted as an orange-red, with the wheel discs in the same colour – the tail was black. The legend Sonnenvogel is depicted as black, but that too is speculative. The wings were covered in five-colour printed camouflage fabric, with light-coloured rib tapes on the lower wing at least. For the planform of this machine and others covered with printed 'lozenge' fabric on the wings, be advised that the choice of the colour of the rib tapes is entirely provisional, as several different colours and patterns were used.

18

Albatros D V (serial unknown) of Oblt Hubertus Freiherr von Rudno-Rudzinski, Jasta 17, Wasquehal, October 1917

At some time in late 1917, Jasta 17 altered its unit marking to a white tail section, but with a black rudder and – usually – black horizontal tail surfaces. Where the usual white Iron Cross border met the white fin, it was often picked out with a very narrow black outline. Both Rudno-Rudzinski and Ltn Wilhelm Becker were photographed in this spectacular D V, named Gisi – it is possible that Becker took it over after 'Rudno' left for Jasta 60. The Gisi legend appeared in white against a black storm cloud, with a 'blitz' marking extending from the last letter. The storm cloud was bordered in a light colour that may have been light blue, grey or even silver. The wings were finished in standard green and mauve camouflage and a flare pistol tube extended from the fuselage beneath the cockpit on the port side.

19

Pfalz D III 1428/17 of Ltn d R Otto Fitzner, Jasta 17, Wasquehal, 30 September 1917

The future ace Otto Fitzner crashed this new Pfalz D III on Wasquehal aerodrome on 30 September 1917, suffering injuries that put him out of action for a month. The Pfalz had probably only just arrived at Wasquehal, and it bore no distinguishing unit or personal markings. Indeed, it had only the usual silver finish and the required factory stencilling. Fitzner returned to Jasta 17 at the end of October, and he would attain his third victory with the unit in March 1918. He left to command Jasta 65 on the 17th of that month. Whilst flying with that unit Fitzner was wounded on 25 August, but soon returned to action and survived the war with nine victories.

20

Albatros D V of Offz Stv Adolf Schreder, Jasta 17, Wasquehal, November 1917

Schreder's D V was decorated with a beautiful 'blitz' insignia emblazoned across the fuselage. This has been interpreted as red with a narrow black border. The D V also displayed the distinctive Staffel marking of a white fin with black rudder and tailplane/elevator. Wings were probably covered in five-colour printed fabric. This colour scheme will be familiar to many readers since a beautiful replica D Va built by The Vintage Aviator Ltd in New Zealand was finished in these markings, with a bit of artistic license. That D Va now resides at Kermit Weeks' 'Fantasy of Flight' Museum in Polk City, Florida.

21

Albatros D Va of Vzfw Brendel, *Jasta* 17, Rethéuil Ferme, December 1917

Vzfw Brendel of *Jasta* 17 has previously been confused with Ltn d R Konrad Brendle of *Jasta* 65, but it is now confirmed that they were two different pilots. *Jasta* 17's Brendel was photographed with this D Va, beautifully decorated with diagonal stripes in a pale colour that we have interpreted as being blue. The background remained in the factory finish of clear-varnished plywood and the tail was painted in the black/white décor of the *Staffel*. There was a rack of flare cartridges on the starboard side of the cockpit and the wings were apparently covered with five-colour fabric.

22

Albatros D Va of Ltn Alfred Träger, *Jasta* 17, Rethéuil Ferme, January 1918

This elegantly decorated D Va is identified as Träger's *'Adler'* ('eagle') in *Staffel* photograph albums, but it cannot be determined if it actually bore that name on its fuselage. It was identified by a detailed eagle insignia in red, and featured the usual black and white tail décor. Five-colour 'lozenge' fabric covered the wings. The author extends his thank to Bruno Schmäling for his information on this and other aircraft details.

23

Albatros D V 4408/17 of Vzfw Georg Strasser, *Jasta* 17, Rethéuil Ferme, winter 1917-18

The most beautiful of Strasser's known machines, this D V is almost certainly 4408/17, perhaps with the insignia repainted over a previous finish. This aircraft was identified by the name *Ly* on the fuselage, which was also elegantly decorated in white with a red heart. It seems to have borne the painted green/mauve camouflage finish on its wings.

24

Albatros D Va OAW (serial unknown) of Ltn d R Alfred Fleischer, *Jasta* 17, Ercheu, June 1918

This was probably Fleischer's first aircraft after he was posted to *Jasta* 17. It had five-colour fabric covering the wings and the usual black/white markings on the tail. The diamonds on the fuselage and Fleischer's 'F' initial were painted in red, and the wheel covers are also provisionally portrayed in this colour as well.

25

Fokker D VII Alb (serial unknown) of Oblt Hermann Pritsch, *Jasta* 17, Vivaise, August 1918

By the time the *Staffel* was equipped with Fokker D VIIs, the unit marking had been changed again. The radiator shells were painted white and the nose was painted an extremely dark colour. The author once believed this was possibly Prussian Blue, but it now seems likely that it was simply black. Pritsch's Albatros-built machine bore unique 'facial' markings around the cooling holes cut into the engine cowling. A broad chevron in a colour thought to be yellow was painted on the fuselage, along with a swastika in the same hue. The enigmatic word *"Bowke!"* (possibly *"Boroke!"*) was painted onto the chevron in black lettering – the significance of this term continues to evade the author. The centre section, undercarriage struts and wheel covers were black as well, while the remainder of the D VII was covered in four-colour fabric.

26

Fokker D VII Alb (serial unknown) of Ltn d R Alfred Fleischer, *Jasta* 17, Vivaise, late July 1918

Fleischer's Albatros-built Fokker displayed unit markings similar to those on Pritsch's machine. The personal markings on the fuselage consisted of yellow(?) borders and a triangular insignia. All struts were apparently left in the factory finish, and four-colour printed fabric covered this aeroplane.

27

Fokker D VII Alb (serial unknown) of Ltn d R Günther Schuster, Vivaise, late July 1918

As the *Staffelführer*, Schuster had his D VII flamboyantly painted in a largely black colour scheme, extended to the fuselage and probably the horizontal tail surfaces too. A personal insignia of a white lightning bolt further distinguished this Albatros-built Fokker, while the wings retained their four-colour fabric finish.

28

Pfalz D XII 1416/18, pilot unknown, *Jasta* 17, Vivaise, September 1918

Jasta 17 acquired a few examples of the Pfalz D XII in late 1918. D XII 1416/18 displayed a factory finish of a dull grey or slightly bluish-grey fuselage and a white fin and rudder. Its nose was finished in typical *Staffel* colours. The personal marking consisted of a white fuselage band, and the tailplane/elevators and wheels were apparently black as well. Five-colour printed fabric covered the wings.

BIBLIOGRAPHY

Bailey, Frank and Christophe Cony, *The French Air Service War Chronology 1914-1918*, London, 2001

Bronnenkant, L, Ph D, *The Imperial German Eagles in World War I, Volumes 1 and 2*, Atglen, PA, 2006 and 2008

Brzenk, Hans, (ed.), *Wir jagten den Feind*, Berlin, 1939

Buckler, Julius (as told to James Perley Hughes), "Wings of Glory No 3: Julius Buckler's Own Story", *War Birds*, August 1934

Buckler, Julius, *"Malaula"*, *Der Kampfruf meiner Staffel*, Berlin, 1939

Cony, Christophe and Bailleux, Yves, "Georg Strasser et la Jasta 17", Parts 1 and 2, *Avions 103 Octobre 2001*, and *Avions 104*, November 2001

Donnell, Clayton, *Osprey Fortress 78 – The German Fortress of Metz 1870-1944*, Botley, 2008

Franks, N, Bailey, F, and Guest, R, *Above the Lines*, London, 1993

Franks, N, Guest, G, and Bailey, F, *Bloody April . . . Black September*, London 1995

Franks, N, Bailey, F and Duiven, R, *The Jasta Pilots*, London, 1996

Franks, N, Bailey, F and Duiven, R, *The Jasta War Chronology*, London, 1998

Grosz, P M, 'The Agile and Aggressive Albatros', *Air Enthusiast No 1*, 1976

Grosz, P M, *Albatros D I/D II, Windsock Datafile, 100*, Berkhamsted, 2003

Grosz, P M, *Albatros D III, Windsock Datafile Special*, Berkhamsted, 2003

Guttman, J, *Osprey Duel 17 – SPAD XIII vs Fokker D VII, Western Front 1918*, Botley, Oxford, 2009

Hamady, Theodore, *The Nieuport 28, America's First Fighter*, Atglen, PA, 2008

Henshaw, T, *The Sky Their Battlefield*, London 1995

Imrie, A, *Osprey Airwar 13 – German Fighter Units 1914-May 1917*, London, 1978

Imrie, A, *Osprey Airwar 17 – German Fighter Units June 1917-1918*, London, 1978

Imrie, A, *Pictorial History of the German Army Air Service*, London, 1971

Imrie, A, *Vintage Warbirds 16 – German Army Air Aces of World War One*, Poole, 1987

Kilduff, Peter, *Hermann Göring, Fighter Ace*, London 2010

O'Connor, N, *Aviation Awards of Imperial Germany in World War 1 and the Men Who Earned Them*, Vols I to VII, Princeton, NJ, and Atglen, PA, 1988 to 2003

Pieters, Walter, *The Belgian Air Service in the First World War*, Marceline, MO, 2010

Revell, A, *British Single-Seater Fighter Squadrons on the Western Front in World War 1*, Atglen, PA, 2006

Revell, A, *Osprey Aviation Elite Units 33 – No 56 Sqn RAF/RFC*, Botley, Oxford, 2009

Rimell, R, *Albatros Fighters Special*, Berkhamsted, 1991

Rimell, R (ed.), *Fokker D VII Anthology No 1*, Berkhamsted, 1997

Sanger, Ray, *The Martinsyde File*, Tunbridge Wells, Kent, 1999

Schäffer, Ernst, *Pour le Mérite, Flieger im Feuer*, Berlin 1931

Theilhaber, Felix, *Jüdische Flieger im Weltkrieg*, Berlin, 1924 (translated by Adam Wait, 1988)

VanWyngarden, G, *Osprey Aircraft of the Aces 77 – Albatros Aces of World War 1, Part 2*, Botley, Oxford, 2007

Wait, Adam (translator) and Norman Franks (ed.), *Julius Buckler: Malaula! The Battle Cry of Jasta 17*, London 2007

Wasenmüller, Karl, "Jasta 17 – Denkschrift über das zweijährige Bestehen der Königl. Preussischen Jagdstaffel 17", *Deutsche Flugillustrierte*, Heft 6, 1935

Zuerl, W, *Pour le Mérite-Flieger*, Munich, 1938

Websites Consulted
www.buddecke.de
www.frontflieger.de
www.theaerodrome.com
www.overthefront.com

ACKNOWLEDGEMENTS

The author owes a very great debt to his friend Adam Wait for his kind permission to quote from his superb translation of Julius Buckler's various accounts, and to Norman Franks for his meticulous research into Buckler's victories and career. The esteemed British historian Trevor Henshaw also graciously shared his in-depth research on British losses matching the victory claims of *Jasta* 17 airmen. German historian Reinhard Zankl generously provided his extensive notes from Georg Strasser's flight log, and Christophe Cony's research into Strasser's career was also extremely useful. The author's deep gratitude, as ever, goes to Tony Holmes and Harry Dempsey for their infinite patience and superb contributions to this book. As always, thanks go to Dieter H M Gröschel, MD, for sharing valuable information from his studies and reviewing portions of the text. Thanks are extended to Lance Bronnenkant and Peter Kilduff for the use of their photographs, and to Jörn Leckscheid and Jon Guttman for their help. The assistance of Manfred Thiemeyer, Bruno Schmäling, Reinhard Kastner, Josef Scott and Alan Toelle is greatly appreciated. The staff members of the History of Aviation Collection in the University of Texas at Dallas were also helpful. Jim Miller, Robert Karr, Dave Douglass, Ray Rimell, Dave Roberts, Justin Young, Eddy Lambrecht, David Mechin, Bernard Klaeyle, Johan Rhyeul, Walter Pieters, Elimor Makavet, Bob Sheldon, Richard Alexander (1914 Aviation Trust) and too many others to name all gave unselfishly of their time and material. The author would be remiss if he failed to acknowledge the contributions of his late friends Rick Duiven, Alex Imrie, Dan-San Abbott, Peter Grosz, George Williams, Neal O'Connor and A E Ferko. The writer's colleagues at *Over the Front* (www.overthefront.com), *Cross and Cockade International* (www.crossandcockade.com), and the *Aerodrome Forum* (www.theaerodrome.com) were also of great help.

INDEX

95